CW00346336

The Sustainable
Careers Handbook

Also by Allan Shepherd

The Kogan Page Guide to Working in the Media
Careers Working Outdoors
Careers Working with Animals
Careers and Courses in Sustainable Technologies

The Sustainable Careers Handbook

Allan Shepherd and
Fiona Rowe

Centre for
Alternative
Technology
Publications

© Allan Shepherd, Fiona Rowe 2000

First published in 2000 by
The Centre for Alternative Technology, Machynlleth,
Powys, SY20 9AZ, UK
Tel. 01654 702400 Fax. 01654 702782
Email: catpub@globalnet.co.uk Web page: http://www.cat.org.uk

The right of Allan Shepherd and Fiona Rowe to be identified as the authors of
this work has been asserted by them in accordance with the Copyright, Designs
and Patents Act, 1988.

All rights reserved. No part of this publication may be reproduced, stored in a
retrieval system, or transmitted, in any form or by any means, electronic,
mechanical, photocopying, recording or otherwise, without the prior permission in
writing of the publisher.

Illustrations: Graham Preston

ISBN 1 89804 925 4
Mail order copies from: *Buy Green By Mail*, Tel. 01654 703409

The details are provided in good faith and believed to be correct at the time of
writing. However, no responsibility is taken for any errors. Our publications are
updated regularly; please let us know of any amendments or additions which you
think may be useful for future editions.

Printed on 100% post-consumer recycled waste by
Biddles Ltd, www.biddles.co.uk

Acknowledgements

Many thanks to all the members of staff at Aberystwyth University careers library: their help has been invaluable. Thanks to all the case studies for passing on their thoughts and experiences: their words have enriched this text considerably. Many thanks to Chloe, and John, Caroline and Graham in the publications department at CAT, and all the members of CAT's amazing information team – various members of which have contributed greatly to the creation of the directory.

The Authors

Allan Shepherd is a BA Hons in Economic and Social History and an MA in International Relations. At university he ran a green group, presented a university radio show, wrote articles for the arts magazine, held down two jobs in local theatres, volunteered at the local radio station and did some academic work.

After graduating he took a job working as a bar manager. An experience yes, a career choice no. He then moved to Wales and volunteered for CAT, where he wrote his first careers book.

For a time he worked as an organic gardener – a rich and rewarding adventure but one that he will probably never repeat. Unable to do just one thing at once, he currently spends three days a week marketing CAT Publications and the other two as a freelance writer.

Fiona Rowe has had all kinds of jobs. She left school straight after taking her O levels and had two children in quick succession. While they were young, she worked on various projects – selling scrap metal, removing and installing cinema seats, running a venue and promoting bands, and writing a regular newsletter. After that, she and her husband spent four years in Canada – alternating childcare with treeplanting. On returning to the UK, she worked for a while in forestry in northwest Scotland, then moved to Edinburgh where she took A levels, and an MA in English Literature and Italian.

After university, she worked as a copywriter, but after a few years realised that she really wanted to do something 'greener', and to work outdoors again. At agricultural college, Fiona took a chainsaw licence course and forestry NVQ, and decided to seek work in woodland management. Having done a work placement at CAT she decided to stay.

She currently works freelance – copywriting and desk top publishing – based at CAT.

Contents

Part Three - The directory

Introduction

Ten years ago a rumour went round my university campus that anyone visiting the careers advisor not knowing what to do with their life would come away with an armful of brochures about accountancy. Luckily, I knew I wanted to be a professional environmentalist – even if I didn't know how I was going to become one. I could visit him without fear, or so I thought... "Ever considered being an accountant in the environmental movement?" He said it with such earnest sincerity I couldn't help but laugh out loud. I laughed so much I had to leave his office. Needless to say I never went back.

I did, however, learn a valuable lesson – never expect to get all the careers information you need from one source. What can be said of even the most clued up and helpful careers advisors can be said of careers books, certainly of this book, which is, essentially, a primer.

We've made no assumptions about who might read this book. You could be a school leaver, a university undergraduate, a downshifter, an entrepreneur, a volunteer, or someone who wants to get out of the job they're in and do something more rewarding. The only assumption we've made is that you share with us a belief that work should be a creative experience that satisfies your needs and those of the planet.

My favourite section of the book is Part 2. This is because it relates real life experiences. We selected twelve people and asked them about their jobs, their lives and their aspirations. The answers they gave could help you decide whether or not a particular job is right for you.

Take this example: "It seems like we work 200 hours a week, but it's probably in the region of 70! Ultimately the buck stops with us and off duty time is restricted – plants can't help themselves to a drink or get up to close the door if there's a bit of a draught." You'll know straight away whether this is you or not.

Each case study is backed up with the information you need to get on.

We tell you what qualifications you'll require, who you can talk to to get advice and which books and magazines are the best to read. When reading the book look out for the symbol (left). It directs you to the relevant page in the directory or other sections. The directory contains the essential details of 359 organisations, 58 magazines and 45 books – all there to help you on your way.

Part 1 guides you from first thoughts to first job. Starting with the basic questions everyone asks themselves at the start of their career it looks at the different employment options, including self-employment and alternative working styles. There are chapters on education and volunteering and a section helping you to get the most out of informal learning opportunities.

The Sustainable Careers Handbook opens the door to a future where your creativity can be used for the benefit of the planet. It is no exaggeration to say that our collective and individual behaviour in the next fifty years will shape its long term destiny and that of the species which have evolved to live on it. Most climate scientists believe we are entering one of the most crucial times in human history. They estimate that worldwide CO_2 emissions need to be cut by 60 per cent to halt the acceleration of global warming. Keeping the planet cool is the number one priority for the 21st century.

Five years ago I wrote a book called *Careers and Courses in Sustainable Technologies*. It was a much slimmer volume. Since then I have seen a tremendous growth of interest in sustainable solutions and a real change in attitudes. Sustainability is no longer a burden but an exhilarating challenge – especially in business, where some companies are starting to win a competitive edge by thinking green. As Dr Alan Knight, OBE (Environmental Policy Controller of B&Q) testifies in his case study on page 84, "I chose this role because it allows me to challenge the paradigm that environment is anti-business. It is not – in fact, done well it is good business."

In *The Next Bottom Line: Making Sustainable Development Tangible*, The World Resources Institute have given business leaders four clear reasons for adopting sustainability as a goal:

- preserving the right to operate by meeting the demands of society;

- reducing cost and liability by making processes cleaner, more efficient, and community-friendly;

- enhancing customer loyalty and market position by taking stewardship for the product throughout its life cycle;

- accelerating revenue growth in new markets for environmentally and socially preferable businesses, products and services.

Some companies have already seen the light. In 1996 Rank Xerox won the European Better Environment Award for Industry for its policy of recovering and re-using old photocopiers. Using its existing network of customers and distribution centres, it collected old machines and sent them to three asset management centres for disassembly and rebuilding. Some parts of the machines go back into new models and others are re-manufactured into new products. By 1995 around 80,000 machines (two-thirds of total output) were remanufactured and sold or dismantled to use as spares. Today the three centres employ 400 people and the company has so far saved about £50 million on the purchasing of virgin raw materials. Non reusable plastic panels were sold for recycling – another net revenue earner. In addition 7200 tones of material did not go to landfill sites, a further saving for the company. As a result Rank Xerox's market share has risen.

It's not just old businesses that are making use of the new thinking. WyeCycle is a good example of a new company doing well because of its environmental philosophy. WyeCycle collects paper, glass, metal, textiles, organic material and garden waste every Monday from homes and businesses in Wye. Households participating in the scheme have reduced their waste to a tenth of the national average and businesses have saved over £10,000 a year in landfill costs. The company gets money from the council because they do not have to dump material in landfill sites and they sell on the collected material. The scheme employs 6 people for a community of 3000. Friends of the Earth have calculated that similar schemes across Britain could create 86,982 jobs.

Local authorities are also starting to meet the challenge. To take one example, local authorities have a duty under the Home Energy Conservation Act to reduce energy consumption by 15 per cent. Although this may mean spending money on a programme of home improvements to housing stock, including damp proofing, insulation and more efficient heating, it can often lead to savings in the provision in health care. Why? Because the home improvements treat the root cause of the problem – poor living conditions and fuel poverty.

Newark and Sherwood District Council, for example, created an £8 million project to improve the energy efficiency of all council housing stock. The programme created an estimated 311 new jobs at a cost of £25,700 per job. However, the council's study also estimated savings to the health service of £2.2 million and savings in unemployment benefit costs of £2.8 million, giving a net cost of just £9,700 per job created.

The same arguments about health and the environment can be applied to the transport industry. According to the Royal Commission on Environmental Pollution, vehicle exhaust pollution in towns and cities is "the prime cause of poor air quality that damages human health, plants and the fabric of buildings". The answer is to increase public transport, encourage cycling and walking and introduce planning policies that reduce the need to travel. Friends of the Earth have calculated that there would be an extra 130,000 jobs as a result.

The Manchester Metrolink Light Railway System is a good example. This new tram system carries over 13 million people in a year, capturing 25 per cent of journeys from car travel in the areas it serves and reducing car trips by 2.5 million a year. Over 1600 temporary jobs were created in construction and 280 permanent jobs in operation and maintenance.

This is a real change in thinking – a quiet revolution creating more job opportunities every year. And this is only the beginning. The UK government is committed by international convention to cut CO_2 emissions by 20 per cent by the year 2010. In their detailed study *Cutting CO_2, Creating Jobs*, Friends of the Earth predict that in four key industries – renewables, co-generation (using waste energy to generate heat), transport and energy efficiency – the number of new jobs created to meet this target will be 236,000. And this figure doesn't include all the other industries featured in this book – organic agriculture and horticulture, ecological restoration, sustainable building, business management and retail, and campaigning and communication – all of which are growing every year.

Of course, the future is never guaranteed and all these predictions are dependent to a certain extent on sensitive government policy and continued public support, not to mention progressive business ideals. Britain is already losing out to other European countries in one sustainable industry – wind power. Despite the fact that Britain has 40 per cent of the European wind reserve, Germany installs more generating capacity (the amount of electricity the wind turbines can produce) in a week than Britain has in the last ten years.

As a result, Germany produces 8 per cent of its electricity from wind power and we produce less than 1 per cent. Denmark does even better; it produces 12 per cent. These countries have capitalised on this growth by creating a whole new industry which manufactures, services and markets wind power technologies. As a result each new generation of turbines is more efficient than the last one and the demand increases once again. We haven't dwelt on the individual performance of each industry featured in this book but we would recommend you find out for yourself by getting hold of the relevant trade magazines.

The Sustainable Careers Handbook will have done its job if it opens the door for you and it inspires you to take control of your future and find work which is creative, rewarding and useful. As the little green fella in *Star Wars* said, "May the force be with you."

Allan Shepherd
August 2000

Part One –
Options at work

Finding the work you want

Knowing what you want from work

Spending your working life doing something you truly believe in will be one of your greatest achievements – because it is one of the hardest battles to win.

So how do you do it...?

The first, and to our minds the most important, step is to look at who you are and what you want out of life. We asked all the people featured in our case studies, "What advice would you give to people reading this book?" A common response was "know yourself, and be true to your own ambitions".

A careers advisor can help you by giving you self assessment questionnaires (you can also get them from the Internet). Although these do not provide definitive career solutions, they do provide a framework for self-analysis. Here are a few examples of the type of question you should be asking yourself.

- Do I like working outside? Some of the people featured as case studies in this book spend most of their time in an office in a city – far away from the natural environment.

- Do I want to take a degree or start work as soon as possible? If you're already fed up with formal education try something else. Starting work is one option, taking a year out – travelling or volunteering (or both) is another.

- Do I worry about money? If financial security is a big thing for you some environmental careers might be difficult. Many environmentalists have sacrificed years of potential earnings to pursue a cause, especially if they are self-employed.

- Do I want to earn a lot of money? One of our case studies earns £60,000 a year but he is unusual.

- Would I be willing to complete monotonous and repetitive tasks as well as interesting ones? Almost all jobs have monotonous and repetitive tasks but some have more than others – farming and building for example.

- Do I like working with people, animals or machines? Some people like to work in a busy office with lots of people around; others prefer contemplative, quiet surroundings.

- What level of responsibility do I want? You could be creating the sustainability policy of a large company or local authority but be prepared to work longer working weeks.

- Am I technologically minded? Solutions can be high tech' or low tech' and both are equally valid. For example, a high tech' solution may save lots of petrol in a motor car, but the low tech' bicycle uses no petrol at all.

- Am I prepared to put up with difficult working conditions? Some people are out in all weathers and others spend a good part of their working day suspended from the blades of bus sized wind turbines.

- What are my main interests? Or, put another way, what excites me? Think about how you can find a job that satisfies your own interests and creativity.

- Do I actually want a career? Some people opt out of the rat race and prefer the experience of travelling, volunteering or trying out lots of different jobs.

Responding to the challenge of global sustainability

Humans impact upon the earth like no other animals. From mum-to-be's car journey to the hospital at the start of life to the funeral procession at the end, humans do things which are bad for the environment. Occasionally we do something positive – like planting a tree – but mostly our activities weaken nature's ability to look after itself. Nappies, toys, school bags, computers, frozen pizzas, beer, condoms, sofas, washing machines, cars, homes, careers books...all are items which take resources from nature and leave behind wastes which pollute it.

Sustainability challenges us to think again about the way we live and work. It poses a difficult question – how can we maintain a high standard of living for all the people of the world without depleting the resources of our natural environment?

Thankfully, the variety of positive responses to the challenge of sustainability is incredibly inspiring. Before you start your search for a career find out about the ideas and people who have gone before and those that live now. There is a rich heritage of colourful characters and ideas to draw inspiration from.

| Example |

Robert Hart's forest garden

Robert Hart was born dead. The attendant doctor revived him, but throughout his life he suffered from ill health as a result of this traumatic entry into the world. In constant pain as a child, he suffered equally in heat and cold. "My whole life has been an Everest ascent," he wrote in the foreword to his book, *Beyond the Forest Garden*. The forest garden is his gift to the world: "a comprehensive answer to two closely related problems: large-scale degradation of the natural environment and the colossal toll of avoidable ill-health." Forest gardening was born of a personal quest to relieve his own suffering, and that of his brother, for whom he cared for many years.

His system of agriculture combines the growing of fruits, nuts, herbs, salad plants and vegetables in a self-sustaining perennial system, which does not require external fertilisers, either man-made or of animal origin. With this system you don't need to plough or dig, which means you don't destroy the soil or deplete it of essential nutrients. It is one step beyond organic growing. Although he designed the system to cope with the British climate he has since discovered that such systems (known as homegardens) exist all around the world – created by peasant farmers for whom a degree of self-sufficiency is essential for survival.

In Hart's words: "Forest gardening offers the potential for all gardeners to grow an important element of their health creating food; it combines positive gardening and positive health...The wealth, abundance and diversity of the forest garden provides for all human needs – physical needs through foods, materials and exercise, as well as medicines, and spiritual needs through beauty and the connection with the whole."

As yet, no one knows how influential Robert Hart's work will be. Organisations like Plants for a Future, as well as countless individuals, are taking his work forward, but forest gardening is still experimental. It is a pioneer idea, as was organic gardening at one time. This, however, does not matter – the facts of his life are inspirational. Despite ill health and pain, Hart patiently tested his theories over a thirty year period – right up until his death aged 86. He didn't even start his experimental work till he was nearly sixty and yet he has left his mark on the world.

All the people featured in our case studies talk about their own setbacks and how they overcame them. As you can see below, the authors of this handbook have done a lot of different jobs – mostly because we were hunting around to find our niche in what can be an incredibly competitive job market. Much of this chopping and changing came from us trying to find out what we were good at and what we really enjoyed doing. At the same time we were assessing how we could best contribute to the process called sustainable development. We had to balance a need to get an income with a wish to see good come from our work.

| Example |

Allan Shepherd

"I discovered environmentalism when I was 19. I watched a Channel Four programme on global warming and it seemed important to me to do something about it, I got involved with my university green group and later went on to run it. It was very creative work but I knew it would be hard to do the same after I left university. I was offered a place on an MA course and took it, because it allowed me to pursue my interest in the environment. I studied the grand sounding subject of the Rational Choice of International Environmental Agreements and left with a good understanding of the political process and how it related to the formation of world treaties. Heady stuff but not that useful in the job market. I got a place to do a doctorate but could not get funding. Retrospectively, this period of time taught me how to organise my thoughts and my work.

"To pay for my MA course I worked in two local theatres, which gave me a good grounding in working life. I ended up managing the bar of one of them which, while not a career move, gave me useful financial and staff management experience. I also worked for a local radio presenter as a programme assistant – an experience which opened up a vista on another side of life.

"Eight months of bar work later I accepted a volunteer placement at CAT and moved to Wales. By this time my CV had started to look a little unconventional.

"After CAT I volunteered at another environmental centre, which was a disaster. I didn't like the work they had given me and I didn't get on with the people there. I was also fed up with working for no money and didn't agree with the aims of the organisation. After four months convincing myself it would get better, I finally decided to move back to Wales, where I started editing and writing careers books for Kogan Page. I also got some paid work at CAT and took on a part-time job at an organic market garden. This business was not a success and I returned to writing.

"Unfortunately, the book projects I spent three months working on fell through and I hit another dead end. Thankfully, I was by now working one day a week for CAT's Publications Department as an editor. This job has grown and I am now the Marketing Officer. For me – and I know a lot of other people are the same – building a career has been a scrappy affair, with lots of stops and starts along the way."

Both the authors of this handbook have followed the steps described as necessary in this book and the steps do work. However they don't prevent setbacks or offer guarantees. Nor do they prevent mistakes. They just set you on the right track and give you a good start. In many ways the setbacks in our careers have been just as important as the positive leaps forward, because they have taught us that sometimes we need to change tack. If your career isn't going in the direction you want it to, you need to stop and think what other options exist and find one that will help you get what you want.

Example

Fiona Rowe

"I've been at CAT for two years now. I first came for a week's work experience as part of a countryside management course, and enjoyed it so much that I came back to volunteer in the gardens. I then found a paid job as telephonist, and am currently freelancing. My next project is more writing work for CAT's display team. I'm certainly not here for the money – none of us are! But it's always been my ambition to live in a beautiful part of the world and work with people whose values I share.

"I've had all kinds of jobs along the way. I left school straight after my O levels and had my two sons when I was 16 and 17. While they were small, I worked with their father at various projects – selling scrap metal, removing and installing cinema seats, running a venue and promoting bands, and writing a regular newsletter, with music reviews and local band gossip. After that, we sold our house and spent four years in Canada, alternating childcare with treeplanting – very hard physical work, but well-paid and in stunning scenery. Other jobs I've had include working on narrow boats, care work, and recruitment consultancy. Retrospectively, two main threads start to emerge – writing and forestry. On returning to the UK, I worked for a while in forestry in northwest Scotland, then moved to Edinburgh. There, I took A levels, and an MA in English Literature and Italian.

"After university, I worked as a copywriter, but after a few years, I realised that I really wanted to do something greener, and to work outdoors again. I went to agricultural college, took my chainsaw licence and forestry NVQ, and decided that after the course I'd work in woodland management. But I did my work placement at CAT..."

Whatever stage you are at in your life your career is always – to borrow a phrase from Hollywood – in development. Some people don't even bother to stop when they reach retirement age. When you start work you must have something to offer the employer – a basic skill or aptitude and a willingness to do the job – but the more work you do the more you learn. As your career develops you build up skills and experiences that will help you in your future work. An unconventional CV, one where the subject has moved between jobs, and sometimes occupations, can demonstrate to an employer an undesirable instability; but it can also show the accumulation of useful working skills and knowledge.

You may have heard the phrase "the glass ceiling". It describes a point in people's careers where a seemingly invisible force prevents them from realising their own potential. It could be a culture of chauvinism, elitism or even racism. With an environmental career there are two glass ceilings. As well as the personal one there is one which stops the world changing. Not only do we have to take ourselves through the glass ceiling, we also have to take our radical ideas through, too. This means that progress towards the world we want is slow.

However, and this is the good news, it is not as slow as it once was, and the speed of change, as our introduction records, accelerates every year. With this in mind, find your own response to the challenge of global sustainability. All the case studies in this book are pioneers: they believe in what they are doing. Out of this belief they create ideas designed to solve the problems caused by the unthinking world.

Finding the job that meets your needs and the planet's

Margaret Thatcher famously remarked that the environment was a "humdrum issue". Nothing could be further from the truth. As Alan Knight, Environmental Policy Co-ordinator of B&Q for 9 years, testifies in his case study:

"I enjoy everything about my job – I achieve things, travel the world – it's interesting, worthwhile and fun. I'm in a position to inspire people with power – buyers, non-governmental organisations and our supply chains – to recognise the importance of social and environmental issues."

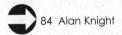 84 Alan Knight

Not everyone wants a high-powered job like Alan Knight, and local responses to the challenge of global sustainability are just as important. David Blair is at the opposite end of the vocational spectrum. He works in semi-natural oak woodland in Scotland. He aims to make the kind of conservation grade product that Alan Knight would consider selling in B&Q. His lifestyle has a minimal impact on the world. He lives very simply and his own personal ecological footprint is small. He doesn't travel all over the world like Alan Knight but he doesn't have the same clout either. This is how he describes his work:

"I work in a beautiful place, I believe in what I do, I – mostly – choose my own agenda, it's creative and it gives me freedom. It's hard graft but I love it. I have never really drawn an income. I use what I need to live and expect to live well."

 96 Dave Blair

There are so many big environmental problems it is hard to know which one to dedicate your life to. Global warming, GMOs, the loss of bio-diversity...the list seems to grow every year and any one problem can make a compelling claim on your time. Try comparing your skills and interests with those of the people in our case studies and see how they made the choices you are facing now. Find something that truly interests you and see how that interest can help the planet. And remember, every problem needs a solution, and someone to find that solution. In the end it doesn't matter how big or small the problem is. The key to global sustainability is a unified intent which allows all people to develop their own responses. The idea of a green funeral is an illuminating example.

Example

Green Funerals

Death is a universal condition, and one that consumes vast amounts of resources every year. Conventional ceremonial trappings of the average funeral may include a tropical hardwood coffin, brass fittings, a granite or marble headstone and thousands of flowers flown in from hot climates. As a response, a company called Vaccari Ltd have created a simple coffin using Sundeala board, which is made from recycled newspaper. The boards are held together with wooden corner joists and wooden nuts and bolts, and organic cloth is used for the lining fabric.

Case study Jenny Hall combines two careers – building and architecture. She is self-employed and accepts contracts of work which may last anything from a few days to a year.

"It's very empowering to be able to build. Physical work means I'm fit and strong. There are negatives too. Building can be a series of boring jobs repeated over and over again. It's important to me that I take on design and drawing as well. My ideal is to work on both the design and building of a project which is ecologically sound."

 76 Jenny Hall

Jenny's pattern of work is found in all sectors of the economy – short term contracts, frequent movement from job to job and even between professions – but some career options are far more stable. Take another of our case studies as an example.

Dave Tobutt is a transport manager with Guildford Borough Council. Part of his job is to investigate options for more environmental vehicles. Although his career has had its setbacks he has steadily risen up through the ranks of the transport industry.

"I have worked in the transport industry for 35 years, with various employers, and have had many setbacks in my career, such as being made redundant and being unsuccessful with job applications. But I got to where I am today because I believed in my own ability to succeed. Of course, I put in a lot of commitment and effort too. I started as a trainee in the workshops and worked my way through the grades, becoming Foreman, Fleet Inspector, Training Officer, Transport Supervisor and finally Transport Manager."

 92 Dave Tobutt

Finding your first job with an employer

It is clear that moving up the ranks is a slow though rewarding process, but one of the hardest tasks can be finding the first job that sets you off on the right path, gives you the experience you need and the confidence that what you are doing is right. The question everyone asks at the beginning of their search for work – and sometimes with a great overwhelming sigh – is where do I begin? Some people work for the family firm, or get a job through a friend but if these options aren't open to you (as is the case for most people) there are three ways of getting a first job with an employer.

1 Be in the right place at the right time.

Lots of people have gone from being a volunteer with an organisation to being a paid employee – even if it is not their perfect job – just by being in the right place when a job came up. The experience in this job helps them to get other jobs.

2 Make a speculative inquiry to a favoured company.

Sometimes you are just what a company is looking for if only it had the time to find you. So find it instead. CAT's own resource guides provide valuable contact names. Also check out magazines, product directories and the Internet for companies working in your field. Getting the approach right is very important. Some people turn up on the door but it is usually better to phone or write first. If you are a school leaver and considering finding a firm who will give you on-the-job training you can get help from your local careers office.

 148 mail order book companies

3 Reply to an advert.

Places to look include national daily newspapers (see box), regional daily and weekly newspapers, local papers, the magazines listed in our directory and of course the world wide web.

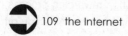 109 the Internet

Get to know the days newspapers print job adverts

Education	*Guardian, Express* (Tuesday), *Telegraph* (Wednesday), *Independent* (Thursday), *Times* (Friday)
Engineering	*London Evening Standard* (Wednesday), *Express, Telegraph* (Thursday)
Environment	*Guardian* (Wednesday)
Finance	*London Evening Standard* (Monday), *Financial Times* (Wednesday/Thursday), *Independent* (Wednesday), *Telegraph, Guardian* (Thursday)
IT	*Independent* (Monday), *Times, London Evening Standard* (Wednesday), *Guardian, Telegraph* (Thursday)
Media	*Guardian* (Monday/Saturday), *Independent* (Tuesday), *London Evening Standard* (Wednesday), *Times* (Thursday/Friday), *Telegraph* (Thursday)
Public Sector	*London Evening Standard* (Monday), *Guardian* (Wednesday), *Times, Telegraph* (Thursday)
Retail	*London Evening Standard, Express, Telegraph* (Thursday), *Times* (Friday)
Sales and Marketing (sometimes fundraising)	*Guardian* (Monday/Saturday), *London Evening Standard* (Tuesday/Thursday), *Express* (Thursday), *Telegraph* (Thursday), *Times* (Friday)

What about self-employment?

Sometimes, to really make a change in the world you have to do it yourself. Look for a niche in the market and make your entrepreneurial talent felt. Although most people have some sort of work experience under their belt before they start their own business, it is not always necessary.

Case study Britta Boyer is a self-employed fashion designer. Her company is called earth 33 and she specialises in materials which have a lesser ecological impact than those conventionally seen in clothes shops. She became self-employed because it was the only way she could make the products she wanted to make.

"I knew I wanted to be a fashion designer from a very early age. The environmental aspect came at a later stage when I developed a conscience about how fickle and wasteful the fashion industry is. I almost gave up my career after completing my degree course and then realised that I may be able to do something positive to change things rather than shun the whole industry."

 88 Britta Boyer

Working alone can be the only sure way to make what you want of your own life but it can be incredibly daunting. It can also be an isolating experience and it is good to have the support of people who care about you and understand the reasons why you are doing the work you are. On the other hand, when it finally pays off, self-employment is very rewarding.

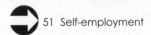 51 Self-employment

Alternative work styles

Some jobs don't really fit into any career structure and are done for reasons of pure belief. Campaigner Patrick Smith gets no income from his work. He explains why in his case study:

"I chose this type of work because it offers me the opportunity to really make a difference, and change opinions. This particular role wasn't always my ambition but I can't imagine doing anything more rewarding than this."

 98 Patrick Smith

There are many people like Patrick – choosing to forego a big wage (or any wage) to pursue cherished values. Many of the most important jobs simply wouldn't get done if traditional economic values were attached to them.

We have included in this book a section on alternative economics. Alternative economic systems help keep local communities together and give individuals a better chance of getting out of unsatisfying, mind-numbing jobs and into creative sustainable employment.

There is obvious economic exclusion in Britain and a whole group of people can't improve their lives because the only access they have to money is through loans from high street banks (which they often find difficult to deal with) or loan sharks, who are waiting to draw blood, sometimes literally, if people default. Talk to someone who works in a Citizens Advice Bureau and they will tell you that a high proportion of their clients have debt problems.

As always, there are solutions to this global problem. In India, small loans are offered to entrepreneurs through a micro-credit system. Without a micro-credit loan many of these people could only work for merchants – who keep the profit for themselves. Micro-credit gives the workers independence and allows them to build up their own businesses. All the money stays in the local economy and extra income from the expanding business is used to feed families, provide health care and get children into school. The interest paid on loans helps other people in the community to take out loans; sometimes whole areas are transformed. Systems where profit is kept by the few to the detriment of the many are unsustainable because poverty prevents progress.

In Britain, small loans can also help people who don't have the time to run the kind of big business a larger loan necessitates, perhaps because they are looking after someone, or they have to do other work just to survive. Sustainability should be all-inclusive and alternative economics play a vital part in this.

 60 Alternative work styles

Working in a co-op

Patrick Smith works in a vegetarian wholefood co-op. Having strength in numbers is very important to the members of the co-op because they face a challenging uphill struggle to get their voice heard but sometimes teamwork is the only thing that will bring a project to fruition. Take this example...

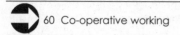

Example

Croissant Neuf Green Roadshow

Since 1994, a troupe of environmentalists and entertainers have been travelling up and down the country throughout the summer, appearing at county shows, carnivals and all kinds of outdoor events. This mobile tour centres around the Croissant Neuf Circus – the world's only wind and solar powered all-human circus. The circus has been showing people of all ages that 'green' can be fun and easy to do.

The Roadshow includes a mixture of workshops, displays, themed entertainment, working models and hands on exhibits that help people understand the problems facing ecosystems. Practical advice from specialists is immediately available for those inspired to change their lives.

60 Co-operative working

Acquiring the skills you need to succeed

Whether you choose to work in a co-operative, a big firm, a local authority or as a self-employed person, you will have to acquire the skills needed to do the job, which basically means you have to think about training and education.

A fair proportion of the jobs described in this book require a university education and some demand postgraduate training on top of that. Each case study describes educational requirements and the chapter on education will help you navigate the system. Reading through all of the case studies will give you a very clear idea of what you can do without a degree. Lots of training could be described as informal – learning on the job, reading up and practicing for example. Read the section on informal learning in the next chapter for some more clues.

Once you have got the training you need – formal or otherwise – you may have to consider a period of voluntary work. Most people in this book have done it and benefited greatly from it. You could start off doing some weekend volunteer work or take a working holiday. Getting in gently is recommended, especially if you have commitments; the chapter on volunteering has some useful pointers and there are plenty of contacts in the directory.

 45 Volunteering

Making the links

Whatever you choose to do and however you choose to work, you should remember that most environmental problems are linked and that we as individuals can quite often solve one environmental problem by tackling another.

> Example

B&Q's sustainable charcoal campaign

Barbeque charcoal is partially burnt wood. Traditionally this wood is taken from coppiced trees (coppicing is a method of cropping which allows the tree to live and grow again). To make more money, some charcoal producers have abandoned the traditional methods and started importing charcoal made from the wood of rainforest trees (which, once cut, die). B&Q found that much of its barbeque charcoal was coming from rainforest trees. They decided to do something about it. Rather than abandon the selling of charcoal altogether they found that they could encourage a new market in British charcoal by buying large quantities from small producers.

The British charcoal makers use only wood cut from the stump so the trees they cut grow again; these trees make an excellent semi-natural woodland habitat of great conservation value. The charcoal is high quality and is sold at a premium. Because it is British it has low transport energy costs. By adopting one sensible development policy, B&Q have provided a valuable market for a British product, helped wildlife and reduced CO_2 emissions.

All of the individual case studies in this book provide the links which enable concerned people to make the connection between the problems they see around them every day and the solutions they need to embrace to solve these problems.

It is easy to write up a scenario that starts with Croissant Neuf and ends with David Blair the woodsman. The circus brings sustainability alive by making it fun; Patrick Smith supplies the real facts behind the fun and points people towards individuals who can help them change their lives. As a result, the new environmentalists want to give their house an ecological renovation. They get Jenny Hall in to do the work and David Blair provides the wood she needs to do the job.

Read the following: it illustrates how the results of our actions are all connected. To the influential American environmental research centre The Rocky Mountain Institute (RMI) it is a guiding parable.

"In the early 1950s, the Dayek people of Borneo suffered from malaria. The World Health Organisation (WHO) had a solution: they sprayed large amounts of DDT to kill the mosquitoes that carried the malaria. The mosquitoes died; the malaria declined; so far, so good. But there were side effects. Among the first was that the roofs of people's houses began to fall down on their heads. It seemed that the DDT was also killing a parasitic wasp that had previously controlled thatch-eating caterpillars. Worse, the DDT-poisoned insects were eaten by geckos, which were eaten by cats. The cats started to die, the rats flourished, and the people were threatened by typhus and plague. To cope with these problems, which it had itself created, the WHO was obliged to parachute 14,000 live cats into Borneo.

"The true story of Operation Cat Drop – now nearly forgotten at WHO – illustrates that if you don't know how things are interconnected, then solutions are often the cause of more problems. On the other hand, if you understand the hidden connections between energy, water, agriculture, transportation, security, and economic and social development, then you can devise a solution to one problem (such as energy) that will create solutions to many other problems at no extra cost."

Taking good care of your self

And finally... Before you set off on your new career, think about how you can maintain your own mental and physical health. There could be a whole new branch of psychology dedicated to environmentalists. Angst, fear, insecurity, depression – none of these conditions are uncommon. You really can feel the weight of the world on your shoulders – especially when society does not appear to be moving as quickly towards change as you would like it to.

There are three important lessons to draw from the experience of others:
- avoid isolation – keep in touch with each other, go to fairs and festivals, help each other out, co-operate on joint ventures;
- do not forget that the mainstream news media is biased towards negative stories – find out what positive things are happening (*Positive News* is a great newspaper for this);
- take good care of yourself – keep fit, eat well and treat yourself regularly to something you fancy.

The following books are a source of inspiration...

Eco Pioneers, S Lemer, The MIT Press, £10.95 This is grist to the mill if you need some more inspiration from people who are already working to reduce the pace of environmental degradation.

Factor Four: Doubling wealth, halving resource use, Ernest Von Weizsacker, Amory B Lovins and L Hunter Lovins, Earthscan Publications Limited, £12.00 pb. A design manual for the 21st Century, this book shows how existing technologies can reduce resource use without threatening standards of living.

Our Ecological Footprint, M Wackernagel and W Rees, New Society Publishers, £11.99 This book helps us define what sustainability is and what we need to do to achieve it. Good luck!

Finding the training you need

Formal education

Education is a bewildering journey. Choosing the right route through the system is the most important thing you can do. A good route can save time and energy. Before you enroll on a course, make sure that it will lead to to a relevant, recognised and properly accredited qualification.

By law, every local authority must employ a careers company to give advice and help. With complete equality, this provision exists to give everyone information and guidance about education, training and employment opportunities. This is the best place to go to find out about the different type of qualifications available to you. Free literature is plentiful – either to take away or read there. Look in *Yellow Pages* to find out where your local branch is.

Read through the case studies that most interest you in this book, work out what qualifications you need and then talk to your local careers advisor about what you want to do. They will do their best to help you get what you want. Go armed with this book and point out what is possible. If you are about to leave school, find out about the Government's training credit. It's available to everyone between the ages of 16 and 18, and it may help you pursue your environmental interests. The money can be spent on academic qualifications, such as A levels, AS levels or GCSEs; or vocational training such as GNVQs, BTEC diplomas and NVQs. It can even help you get on an apprenticeship scheme.

| Example |

Ecobuilding
Ecobuilders apply conventional skills to sustainable ends. They can receive training through college courses or learn their trade on the job. At the present time there is no standard NVQ qualification for sustainable building but there are NVQs for general skills which teach you

the nuts and bolts of the job. If you want to be an ecobuilder, and you want to train on the job, you may be able to persuade a local builder to take you on as a trainee.

Environmental builders have their own professional organisation – the Association of Environment Conscious Building. They produce a directory with all their members' names and addresses. This might help you find a local builder who could be interested in taking you on as a trainee. The local careers office can help you negotiate with the builder and get a good deal for both of you. You get a mixture of on the job and college training and he/she gets an apprentice to help do the work.

Is a degree necessary?

A degree is not necessary for building but it is for architecture and many other jobs listed in this book (each case study includes educational requirements).

Anybody wanting to take a Higher National Diploma, Diploma of Higher Education or a first degree at a British university or college must apply through UCAS (Universities and Colleges Admissions Service); the *UCAS Handbook* is an essential, and free, acquisition (your local careers library should have one, or you can get one from the address listed in the directory). Apart from listing all full-time and sandwich courses, it offers guidance to the application procedure. It does not however list entrance requirements. For this information you need to consult *University and College Entrance: The Official Guide*, the UCAS website, or the colleges and universities themselves. All educational establishments will send out their prospectus free of charge. These are essential. Courses can vary quite considerably so you should get a whole bunch of them, stack them up in a pile and go through them all one by one. Alternatively, log on to university websites (most have direct links with individual departments).

You will need to do all this research a long time before your first term. Applications must be submitted between 1st September and 15th December in the year before the course starts. As UCAS acts as a clearing house for universities, passing on applications to be considered by individual departments, it is best to get your application in earlier, rather than later; as the deadline approaches applications take longer to process. Late applications will still be considered by universities but offers will only be made if places aren't filled. All applicants listing Oxford or Cambridge must apply by 15th October. If you are applying for an art and design course the rules are different again. Check the *UCAS Handbook* for details.

 140 careers help

A degree should allow you access to better paid jobs but employers quite often want to know that you can do the job before you start. Often you need a degree, experience and a postgraduate qualification. Some degrees include a year's work experience in their normal training programme. You get to see inside a company and meet people who might offer you work when you graduate.

Contact the National Centre for Work Experience for details.

 141 working holidays and gap year experience/books

Postgraduate qualifications allow an advanced level of study that normally includes an interesting research project. Quite often these projects are of interest to companies developing new products or services and you can sometimes get funding for them. *The Prospects Postgraduate Funding Guide* is recommended by the Association of Graduate Careers Advisory Services.

 145 postgraduate funding

Apart from the *UCAS Handbook*, the most essential publication to get hold of is the Environment Council's *Directory of Environmental Courses*. Published every two years, it is a complete guide to academic, professional and vocational courses related to the environment.

The fifteen subject areas it covers are agriculture, architecture, building and housing studies, environmental education, environmental engineering, environmental law, environment management, environmental studies and ecology, forestry, horticulture, industry and the environment, local management studies and conservation, landscape architecture and design, surveying, urban planning and management. Every careers office should have one as it is sent to them automatically.

If you haven't done so already you should also get on the world wide web. UCAS have their own site (www.ucas.ac.uk) but you should also check out www.careersworld.net which is excellent. From here you can link to the website of any British university. There is also a database of courses and articles, including reports on student life. Gap years and modern apprenticeships are also covered. Go to Yahoo (a powerful website that searches other websites for you) and type in careers. At the last count there were 119 relevant sites in Britain alone. A list of some of these sites can be found in the directory on page 111. If you want to check out what postgraduate courses are available in Britain, visit www.prospects.csu.man.ac. You will find at least 70 relevant courses with the word sustainable in their title and many more using the word "environment".

Informal and additional learning

Formal education teaches you the nuts and bolts of a skill. How to use a spanner. How to draw technical diagrams and so on. Sometimes it teaches you how to apply those skills to work which is sustainable. Most of the time however it does not. Consequently the majority of people don't know how to apply the skills they have learned through formal education in a way which will help the planet – in fact quite the opposite.

Most car designers make petrol driven vehicles, most builders construct to the minimum standards of energy efficiency, most plumbers don't know how to install a solar water heating system.

This section is about how to make the switch – it tells you how to find the information you need to practise your skill, art or craft sustainably; it is written for those of you who have already learned a trade, those of you who feel your courses don't teach you what you really want to know and for those of you who are choosing a course at the moment.

Funding your degree

With the phasing out of student grants it is now almost inevitable that you will leave university with a large debt. Each year, you will have to take out a loan to pay for living expenses. In 1999/2000 this figure was £3,635 (£4,480 if you live in London). However, you won't have to start paying off the debt unless you start earning over £11,000 per annum (year 2000 figures), and then the interest payable is linked to inflation, not normal bank rates. On top of this, students are expected to make a means tested contribution to their tuition fees (maximum £1,025 per year).

The only professional qualification exempt from this system is the Postgraduate Certificate in Education, PGCE, (for teachers), for which there is financial support. In addition you can apply for hardship grants and, if you are disabled, a Disabled Student Allowance (DSA). The Department for Education and Employment publishes a very useful guide, *Financial Support for Students – a guide for those starting in higher education*. Phone 0800 731 9133, or if you are using a textphone, 0800 210 280.

Sponsorship may be one answer to this problem, or a grant from a trust. Neither of these options are readily available though. Grants are sometimes made to students who meet particular criteria. *The Directory of Grant Making Trusts* is the book to get hold of and most libraries have a copy. If they don't, get them to order it for you. This service incurs a minimal charge.

 145 funding

- Join one of the environmental organisations listed in the directory. Membership organisations save you massive amounts of time because they give you access to vast amounts of information. Most of them produce a magazine and relevant publications which will help you. Some may put you in touch with fellow members who would be prepared to give you advice. Others need volunteers.

- Find out what books are available. If the course you are currently studying doesn't for example teach you how to put a wind turbine together buy a book that will. Get catalogues from companies specialising in sustainable books and read up on the relevant subjects.

148 mail order companies

- See if you can take a specialist course. There are hundreds of small courses relating to sustainability that don't lead to a qualification but teach you basic skills – the idea being that you go away with your new skill and practice. The relevant organisation will be able to point you in the right direction.

- Contact a professional organisation in your chosen field – they may already have a unit set up to deal with enquirers like you.

- Subscribe to the relevant magazines. Not only can this help you keep up with current events, it also gives you access to valuable technical information.

- Purchase resource guides from CAT and write to the companies listed to check vacancies. You may be able to start as a trainee and learn the skills you need – either supported through a government scheme, or independently as a kind of apprentice.

 173 CAT publications

- Attend "green" fairs and festivals. Summer festivals are good places to learn. As well as finding out about relevant organisations, you can often participate in practical workshops. Although these only teach the basics, they do provide a good free entry point to unusual careers. You may find yourself, for example, enjoying the gentle spin of the pole lathe or potter's wheel rather more than you might have first imagined you would.

- Use the internet. If you don't have a computer, most public libraries do. There will always be someone on hand to help you if you get stuck. The Internet is a vast world library that anyone can visit.

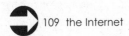 109 the Internet

- Teach yourself through practical projects, either alone or with a co-op; this is obviously easier for something like building and gardening than it is for waste management.

- Volunteer.

Volunteering

Working for free! Doesn't sound very good, does it, but volunteering is an easy way to learn about the job you want to get paid for doing. In fact, sometimes it is the only way. Most of the people featured in this book have been, at some point in their life, volunteers – even if it was only for a weekend. Some of them say a long period of voluntary work was an essential experience. Others note that it broadened their horizons and gave them an opportunity to meet people who changed the course of their lives.

> Example

Steve Ward – Energy Projects Manager, Intermediate Technology Consultants

Steve took up a six month volunteer placement at the Centre for Alternative Technology after graduating from the University of Warwick with an engineering degree. As a volunteer he helped maintain a renewable energy system – receiving valuable training from specialists. After six months he successfully applied for a placement with renewable energy company Dulas Ltd. This eventually led to a full-time job within their micro-hydro department. The knowledge acquired as a volunteer at CAT helped Steve win a placement at Dulas, who were looking for someone with some experience.

So there it is – the perfect formula: education + voluntary experience = paid work in a plush job.

If only it worked like that every time! Volunteering does not offer any guarantee of work and can lead to disappointment and frustration if your hard work for free isn't met with immediate rewards. Even worse there is another dark side to volunteering. The actual experience of volunteering isn't always positive. Choosing the wrong organisation, the wrong project or the wrong person to give up your time for can be a very negative experience.

Example

The best of times or the worst of times

If you want to get experience of organic growing, you can join an organisation called Willing Workers on Organic Farms (WWOOF). As a member, you can go to work on a smallholding or farm. There are farms all over the country and you can choose whether you want to work with animals or vegetables. A weekend at one of these farms can be a rewarding and interesting experience. Hosts provide free food and accommodation and volunteers help them do basic work.

If you have no experience of organic growing you can pick up a lot of information quickly. For some people this is the ideal way to learn about organic growing and lots of fun. Both authors of this book have been on WWOOFing weekends and would recommend it but there are some horror stories. Some WWOOF hosts have been asked to leave the organisation because they treat volunteers badly – sometimes as free labour, often providing inadequate accommodation and, ironically, poor food. The organisation will act on a complaint, but you might be the one making it.

So how do you avoid the negative experiences? There are no guarantees that you can avoid them but there are some sensible precautions:

- always find out as much about an organisation as possible before you go;

- ask what their aims are and make sure they match your own personal ambitions;

- never commit yourself to long periods of volunteering unless you know the set-up well. This usually means spending a few days there first;

- always ask for written details of the arrangements for volunteering. These details should explain the work you will be doing, how many hours a week you are supposed to work and what benefits you will receive. If an organisation doesn't have anything in writing, ask them why;

- if you can, ask others if they know what the organisation is like;

- always remember volunteers are free to leave at any time. Contracts are very unusual for volunteers but if you are asked to sign one, and are not happy about it, ask the Citizens Advice Bureau to check it for you.

The most essential rule of volunteering is – don't spend too much time doing it! Six months to a year is about the most anyone should do – unless you know that it will definitely lead to paid work. Much more than this and you start to feel you'll never get just rewards for your time and effort. At some point you've got to decide in your head that you are no longer a volunteer.

We should qualify this by saying that millions of volunteers give up their time regularly each week over a longer period because it is fun and rewarding and because the work provides valuable social contact. If you are getting a lot out of volunteering, and if it is something you really believe in, then why give it up?

Sometimes volunteering can run alongside other work. 'Doing' the festival circuit is one way. Spending your weekends camped out in the sun (or mud), you could be signing up revellers for Greenpeace membership or staffing the Water Aid toilets at Glastonbury or just running a stall; there are plenty of options and lots of work to be done. If you have a campaign, take it to the fair.

| Example |

Ecotrip

Ecotrip is a green action and education group. Those involved have backgrounds in protest, campaigns and networking centres and aim to bring lessons and experiences to a wider green audience, thereby encouraging more people to get involved in grassroots political change. During the summer Ecotrip tour the festival circuit doing workshops on a wide range of green topics. Their marquee provides a comfortable space with carpets and cushions for people to talk, eat and browse through the information sheets and books available.

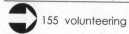 155 volunteering

Work experience

A work experience programme is another option. Although this is slightly different to volunteering (as you may get paid for doing it), it follows the same principles. Whether you are at school or university, time spent doing work experience can really boost your confidence and open up new avenues of work. More importantly it shows potential employers that you have spent some time in a working environment – fitting in with normal working procedures and building up your teamworking, communication and interpersonal skills. For full details contact the National Centre for Work Experience (see page 140 for address) and ask for their publication *Focus on Work Experience*. Their website is www.ncwe.com.

Living while volunteering

This is a tricky conundrum. By law you can't volunteer a full week's work and sign on. You can only sign on if your volunteering activity amounts to less than 16 hours a week. If you are volunteering more than 16 hours a week the Government, ironically, believes that you are not actively seeking paid employment – even though this is your long term aim.

There are exceptions to this rule and they come under the rules of the so-called New Deal. If you are aged between 18 and 24, you can sign up for the Government's New Deal programme. There are four options:

• a job with an employer who receives a government subsidy for six months or you may get help with setting up your own business,

• work with the Environment Task Force to improve the environment of your community,

• work in the voluntary sector,

• full-time education or training geared to helping you into work.

If you work for a voluntary organisation or the Environment Task Force you are guaranteed at least the equivalent of the Job Seekers Allowance (JSA), plus a grant of up to £400 paid over 26 weeks. For more information call 0845 606 2626 or visit the New Deal website at www.newdeal.gov.uk. You may also find an organisation to pay basic living costs and provide you with food and accommodation. This will allow you to sign off and pursue your ambitions.

If you are starting up your own business you may be able to get grants to cover start up costs while you volunteer your time for free. The Shell Better Britain Campaign produces a magazine with regular lists of grant makers.

Starting your own business

Environmentalists are entrepreneurs by nature. They come up with practical solutions to difficult problems and take great risks to fulfil a personal vision. They invest time and energy into ideas which are unproven and put off the rewards of their work for years to come. They have always been willing to 'get on their bikes'. And yet strangely this entrepreneurial spirit has only slowly made its presence felt in the business world.

One of the reasons for this is that demand for some of these innovative ideas is only now equalling supply. From organic food to clockwork radios the clamour for ecoproducts and services has never been greater. Consumers aren't just interested, they're excited. This is very good news for the small trader with a good idea.

Example

Hemp Union

Cannabis, or hemp, is a plant with a bad reputation. Smoke it as a drug and you are breaking the law. However, turn it into cloth and you have a British grown alternative to cotton (cotton can only be grown in hot countries thousands of miles away). Grow it organically and you have an ecological vote winner, especially as the hemp variety used to make products will not get you high! Hemp can also be used as an oil, as a seed in cooking, as a building material (hemp fibre board and hemp bales), as an ingredient in cosmetics...the list isn't endless but it could certainly fill a few more lines of this book.

Hull based Hemp Union – set up originally to fulfil a demand for ecological clothing – have developed a wide range of products, including oils, snack bars and stationery. They now stock the widest range of hemp related products available from a UK retailer – bigger even than the Body Shop (for whom they acted as a consultant). As well as retailing, Hemp Union assists growers and works with engineers, chemists, nutritionists and farmers to come up with new products.

Self-employment sometimes seems like the easy option but it isn't. Many people believe that no boss = no hassle, but the self-employed person has numerous bosses – the client, the bank manager, the tax man, the health and safety inspector, the trading standards officer, the local council, the government.

As a sole trader, you have to deal with everyone and, unlike regular employment, you aren't protected in the same way by the law. No paid holidays, no limit to the number of working hours in a week, no easy tax payment scheme, no sickness pay, no minimum wage. All costs have to be covered by the prices you set. Not only do you have to do your job, you have to do other people's jobs too – filing, typing, accounts, marketing, distribution (i.e. driving the van) and so on.

We asked case study Chris Laughton, a self-employed energy advisor, what his weekly work entailed. This is his reply:

"For about 4 days a week, it's finding potential customers, visiting prospective projects, preparing design and costs, organising tools, materials and workers, on-site construction, and paperwork. Roughly one more is spent on technical data, storage and stocking of materials, creating artwork, finance forecasting, tool/vehicle maintenance, scouring trade journals/the internet, computer upgrades/training, and paperwork. Occasional work includes presentations, media work, and photographs and paperwork. Oh, did I mention the endless paperwork? Actually it's mostly done on the computer but it's still very tedious."

But at least you have absolute creative freedom to do what you want. Make a table out of old spoons – yes. Manufacture tipis – yes. Spend your days collecting driftwood from sandy beaches and transforming them into table lamps – yes, yes, yes. Well, you can if you have the market for them. To make up an adage, it ain't going to gel if it ain't going to sell. So the first rule of making self-employment work is – find your market and pursue it relentlessly.

Small business advisors recommend the following as good business sense.

- Always organise your thoughts and actions. This saves time and energy.

- Think about yourself. Will you enjoy self employment? Can you cope with insecurity and setbacks?

- Think about the product or service you want to sell. Who will buy it? How will you sell it? What resources do you need to produce it?

- Make a business plan. Work out how much money you need to start up and run the business until you make a profit. Set sales targets – how much business you need to do to pay off the loan and earn enough to live.

- As management strategists suggest, "walk through the plan in 3D". Ask yourself – will I be able to fulfil my plan in practical terms? Are there enough hours in the day? Will my supplier be able to sell me the stuff on this day so that I can sell it on to my customer the next day?

- Find the money. This is probably one of the hardest tasks. Ecological businesses can apply for loans from the Ecology Building Society and from Triodos Bank, but you could also see if there is a local credit union to borrow from (small amounts only but with favourable terms). Also try The Prince's Trust (they offer business loans at favourable rates) or a normal high street bank.

If you don't want to get a loan you may be eligible for a grant – but these tend to be aimed at community groups rather than individuals. Check out the *Directory of Grant Making Trusts* in your local library. Subscribe to the magazine of the *Shell Better Britain Campaign* as they have a regular round-up of new grants. Grants like these usually cover start up costs but rarely wages. One example of this is the start up grant given by Environment Wales for small group enterprises in Wales. Another useful publication is the *Environment Funding Guide*, published by The Directory of Social Change.

145 grants and loans

- Find out exactly what legal responsibilities and duties you have as a self-employed person. Buy a book on working for yourself. You will have to learn how to do basic bookkeeping as well, even if you have an accountant to do your final tax returns.

 148 for publishers' addresses

- Talk to people who can help you. Visit your local Business Link officer (every region will have one – there are 87 in all). The central helpline (0345 567765) will put you in touch with your nearest office. They will also send you a brochure on request, outlining how to start and where to get help. The Business Link Officer is there for people like you and they are very willing to help – however unusual the request. The DTI (Department of Trade and Industry) also produce an information brochure – *Setting up in Business*. Call 0870 152500 and quote reference URN 99 833.

You could also contact Shell Livewire, and your local Citizens Advice Bureau, Job Centre, Training and Enterprise Council (Local Enterprise Company in Scotland), Local Enterprise Agency (Trust in Scotland), council or careers office. If you live in Wales, Scotland or Northern Ireland you should also get in touch with your regional development board. There are also special bodies to help rural and community businesses.

 137/152 business innovation and positive economics

- Find out if there are any local courses on running your own business or on related skills you may need to acquire, like bookkeeping, using a computer or marketing.

- Have a look at what books are available on general business success. Many environmentalists have shunned mainstream business practices without really understanding that these can be used just as much to enhance their own aims. Having a good sound knowledge of business can give you the competitive advantage over non-green products. A classic text to get hold of is *Marketing Without Advertising* by M Phillips and S Raspberry.

Even if you've got all the elements right it can still take a few years to become a really effective business. Freelance fashion designer Britta Boyer set up her business, earth 33, when she became disillusioned with the fashion industry. She told us how hard it has been to make her work pay:

"As a sole trader I have had to work very hard – anywhere between 40 and 80 hours a week. I do the bookkeeping, administration (paying bills and answering the phone!), sales, PR, organising production, delivering collections on time to retailers, and I spend a limited amount of time designing and planning future collections. I would advise anyone who does the same to expect very little income for at least two years – if not longer. I have had to work other jobs to support myself. I have read and heard from other businesses that you do not start seeing a return for about five years and after the seventh you have a potential to make a good profit and a healthy income. In this time I have had to live a minimalist lifestyle. I do not regret this but it can get me down, as does the loneliness of running your own business."

Is small still beautiful?

Small is Beautiful is the name of a book written by Fritz Schumacher (first published in 1973). The phrase became an environmental slogan and a rallying cry against the inhumanity of modern industrial technologies and the techniques of mass production. Schumacher wanted what he called intermediate technology – technology that people could control, understand and fix themselves. He argued for human scale development and economics that kept the profit of work within the community, and that the giganticism of the multinational company was fundamentally flawed because it was out of proportion to the human scale. The only way to solve the environmental crisis was to go small.

Thirty years on, the world has changed. For one thing, we think in terms of the global village, of a community stretching across continents. For another, mass production technology has shown that it can be a force for good. Although most of us would not know where to begin when fixing a computer, we do not underestimate its value – in deciphering environmental messages from changing natural systems, or in saving energy, or in creating models that can help us find better ways of doing things. The most compelling difference however is that some large companies are actually profiting from being good.

This new world has created a dilemma amongst some environmentalists – whether to work for big companies and achieve big things, while risking a kind of ethical contamination, or keep small and beautiful. We also have to ask the question after years of free-range planetary profiteering: can we trust large multinational companies to change the world they created or do we need to do it ourselves? While big may be quicker and faster, is it better? Or is small still beautiful?

This chapter looks at the two extreme ends of the industrial scale – the gigantic and the minute – to see where an ethical dimension fits into the process of sustainability. If you have an ethical objection to the business practices of large companies, or if you prefer the idea of small scale community action, it offers examples of some of the alternatives.

Multinationals

Multinationals – does anyone like them? In the last few years multinationals have become the focus of much "ecowrath" – not least because they behave like unelected governments over whom we have no control. On the other hand, they produce items few of us could easily live without. In many ways we are victims and beneficiaries of a system that ultimately ties us all together. Two of the biggest companies developing renewable energy, for example, are the oil producers BP and Shell. Sometimes the case is more clear cut. McDonalds, for example, generate what can be called an unsustainable product with no positive impact on the environment. They were recently in court for what turned out to be the longest libel case in history.

| Example |

Burger culture on trial

In the most famous libel case of the century, McDonalds, fighting as Goliath against the self-defending libellers Dave Morris and Helen Steel, were found to

- be "culpably responsible for cruel practices in the rearing and slaughter of some of the animals used to produce their food" – statement made in leaflet *What's wrong with McDonalds* and upheld by Mr Justice Bell;
- "exploit children by using them as more susceptible subjects of advertising" – Mr Justice Bell;
- "pay low wages and depress wages for other workers in the industry in Britain" – John Vidal's interpretation of Mr Justice Bell's judgement, in his book *McLibel – Burger Culture on Trial*.

In this court case, the two defendants couldn't prove their claims that McDonalds destroyed rainforest and were "wrecking the planet".

What can be said of all multinationals is that they have the potential to stamp a large ecological footprint on the earth. Even though McDonalds weren't responsible for "wrecking the planet", they couldn't argue that their business did not use large amounts of non-reusable resources.

But what can also be said of large multinationals is that they have an amazing potential for good; any positive change is likely to be enormous. A company which has made sustainable development a priority can apply their principles on a very large scale. A person who chooses to work for an organisation that has made such a commitment can make a big impact in turn through their work.

Some big businesses are in a very good position to implement technological changes which will cut pollution substantially. Being at the heart of such a business could be a rewarding experience, and one that combines a good income with high job satisfaction. Materials scientists, engineers, retail managers and a host of other professionals all have a part to play.

| Example |

B&Q

B&Q are often quoted as being world leaders in the area of sustainable development. Prompted by media and consumer interest, the company started an environmental programme in 1990. The board of directors were convinced that sustainability was becoming a business issue and set about creating a programme which they hoped would add value to their own products, save money and help the environment.

Ten years on and the results are quite amazing. Not only have they cut waste and saved energy in their own stores, they have introduced better working conditions for employees in developing countries, where many of their products are sourced, and have introduced a green agenda for all their products.

Some of the measures have been quite simple, showing dramatic returns quickly. For example, B&Q toilet seats were once packaged in a polystyrene tray. The simple removal of this tray has saved the company £100,000 a year. The company also sets standards in honest reporting. In their report *How Green is My Patio?* they acknowledge that they are not a green company, but state that they are working towards this. With immense spending power they can be a force for good, and a reflection, they feel, of their own customers' concerns.

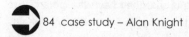 84 case study – Alan Knight

The real problem with working for a big multinational group is that you may unwittingly be generating profits that another company within the group uses to do something you disagree with; for example supporting a government that suppresses democracy; or condoning poor working conditions for employees in other countries; or making an incredibly harmful product.

Many large companies also dominate the world's political agenda, which makes them seem less accountable. The Multinational Agreement on Investment (MAI) was drawn up to give international companies unprecedented powers to protect their own interests at the expense of domestic legislation. Thankfully, due to popular protest culminating in the Battle for Seattle (the biggest popular demonstration against multinationals and the international organisations which support them), the agreement has been put on hold. If it does come into force large companies will be able to object to domestic, environmental and social welfare measures on the grounds that they are a restriction to free trade.

Separating truth from fiction is quite a problem when it comes to finding out if a big business is ethically sound. There are several important sources of information (all magazines) – *Corporate Watch, Ethical Consumer, New Internationalist, The Ecologist* and *Green Pepper*. If you do want to work for a big business it is worth finding out about the company first. Get their prospectus and see if they make any environmental claims. If they do, check that they are true by reading the reports produced by *Ethical Consumer*.

The Worker Co-operative

One way of avoiding some of these ethical dilemmas is to form or join a co-op. A co-op is an organisation created on a human scale. Its members have consciously chosen to practice a principle of equality. There are some obvious advantages:

- members find the atmosphere invigorating and, because everyone has the opportunity to speak out about an issue, there is a genuine feeling of participation;

- skills can be shared to achieve a common goal;

- skills are valued equally;

- the co-op structure can allow for the blossoming of good ideas which may in other companies wilt under the sour gaze of a critical senior manager;

- co-operatives can bring small amounts of money together to make a pot of money big enough to get a project off the ground.

Smaller co-operatives have a flat management structure. Decisions which affect the whole co-operative are taken at regular meetings with most of the members of the co-op present. As a co-op becomes bigger, it often becomes impossible for this decision-making structure to run smoothly. As a result a second tier of management is devised and members elect a core team to make decisions with their approval. Also when co-ops grow bigger it is not always possible to maintain equal wages for all.

| Example |

The Centre for Alternative Technology

The Centre for Alternative Technology is a worker co-operative which has evolved its own particular structure. There are 36 permanent members of staff, all on the same wage – engineers, fundraisers, builders, gardeners and so on – and, depending on the time of the year, between 10 and 40 contracted and casual staff (on a lower wage).

Each month the whole co-op meets to make important strategic decisions and every week a smaller group, elected from the body of members, meets to consider matters arising from day-to-day business. There is a lobbying system for all staff and any permanent staff member can object to a decision and ensure it is discussed by all. In this way everybody has some say.

The co-op system is not perfect however and anyone wanting to start one should think carefully about some of the disadvantages:

- if you have a particularly individual vision you may not be able to or want to share it with others. Co-operatives work best where there are small numbers with an agreed and shared vision;

- decision-making can be slow and as a co-operative structure is more inclusive people need to be consulted before decisions are made. If you don't like this sort of consultative process then a co-operative may not be for you;

- their openness is sometimes counter-productive; because members can argue their point, arguments can be frequent and opinions frankly given. This sometimes leads to the more confrontational or outspoken members getting their own way;

- although the structure is more inclusive it still has its share of office politics; all workers are nominally equal, but, like George Orwell's fictional pigs in the novel *Animal Farm,* some are more equal than others.

The housing and worker co-operative

Some people combine home and work life together by joining or forming a housing and worker co-op – which in environmental terms makes a lot of sense as you don't have to travel to work. Co-ops make housing affordable. The members of the co-op own the house but pay rent to the co-op. The co-op carries the risk of the mortgage and none of the members are personally liable if the co-op defaults on payment. This is ideal in situations where individual members can't get a mortgage themselves – they may be in temporary work or unemployed – but want to live in a house which isn't owned by a landlord.

A few housing co-ops have managed to secure land to work. One of the most famous is Tinker's Bubble in Somerset.

| Example |

Tinker's Bubble

A group of people bought some land and set up low impact dwellings. They started to work the land, making coppice products from a few acres of woodland, for which there was a ready market in the local area. As planning permission for dwellings had not been granted the council asked them to leave. They argued their case and eventually won a famous victory; they were allowed to stay because their project was a good example of low impact sustainable development.

There are many different sorts of communities, communes and networks in the UK. It is possible to go and stay with some of these, either as a weekend "guest" or as a permanent member. However, since each one has a distinctive aim it is well worth doing some research into what exists. It is important to know whether they would suit you, or for that matter, whether you would suit them!

Every year the Communes Network publishes *Diggers and Dreamers* – an independent guide and directory to British communes/communities (plus numerous international contacts). It explains how to visit, join, live and work in a community.

Worker co-operatives have a long history and there is plenty of information to be had from the various sources listed in the directory. You can find out how to set one up and run it, and how to form links with other co-ops.

 34 for information on co-ops

Community bartering

Everyone wants to get lots of money for their work. Right? Wrong. Some people in Leicestershire prefer to swap their labour for "beans". They are the members of a Local Economic Trading Scheme (LETS). Everyone knows that Jack got into trouble for swapping his cow for beans but it turned out all right in the end because the beans grew into a giant stalk and he found lots of money. Well, LETS schemes are a bit like that. Except, rather than ending up with a giant stalk and lots of money, members help each other by supplying essential goods and services at the same rate.

Example

The lawyer, the pumpkin and the masseur

A lawyer might want to buy a giant pumpkin for his daughter's halloween party. His neighbour needs some legal advice, and his neighbour's friend has a giant pumpkin for sale. In the money economy the value of the pumpkin would be much much less than the value of the legal advice but in the LETS scheme it has the same value. So the lawyer "buys" the pumpkin for 3 beans, which he earned giving the neighbour some legal advice. The gardener spends her beans on a massage – after growing such a big pumpkin she deserves it!

In total there are nearly 450 LETS schemes in Britain. The more established schemes include local authorities and shops. The system builds links between people and helps to support communities; for individuals it is a valuable opportunity for improving their quality of life.

 153 LETS schemes

Credit Unions

Credit Unions are an ethical alternative to banks. The money members invest is used to boost the local economy and to help individuals or groups who do not have the access they need to large banks. It is also a response to loan sharks, who charge hiked-up interest rates for small loans, often leaving the borrower owing more in interest than the value of their original loan. They work by helping the 1.5 million households who do not have access to mainstream financial services.

Individually, members do not have a great deal of financial clout, but as a union they can strike good deals with large companies; this can save considerable amounts of money for the group as a whole. There are now 650 credit unions in Britain, with total assets of £124 million.

 152 credit unions

Poverty prevents progress and the cause of poverty is unshared wealth. Mahatma Gandhi believed that we should live simply "so others should simply live". A credit union is one response to the problem of poverty; another is income sharing. Income sharing groups developed in Britain in the seventies as a response to greedy consumerism.

Sharing resources

Group members pool wages and distribute them equally amongst the group; what they actually put into the pot in the first place doesn't matter. If someone is unable to earn one week they don't go hungry, they don't lose their home, they don't become indebted to loan sharks or pawn brokers.

The group also acts as a brake on consumerism; a conscious financial planning process ensures that individuals do not spend recklessly. Members consume less and work less. They have more free time to pursue interests outside work.

Example

Snowball

The *Guardian* reports, "Part-time management consultant Guy Simmons earns £322 a week – yet every time he needs a new shirt for work he has to get the agreement of five other people." Guy Simmons is part of Snowball, a group opposed to capitalism and consumerism. With the other five members he pools his funds and joins in with the weekly meetings to see how the money should be spent. Their combined incomes pay for food, rent and household bills and each member gets a pocket money allowance of £17.50. Special purchases are discussed openly and there are rarely disagreements. This is because their common aim is mutual support. Each member is mindful of the others when making a request.

Example

Give and Take

"Pop down the market and pick up a hi-fi, or a £500 coat, or a video recorder, or a bike, or a lawn mower, or a set of tools, or even a set of four solar water heating panels! And take that microwave we never use – all for free." For free, are they mad? No. Just part of the Well Health group – a group set up to make a human scale challenge to wealth. Well Health's Give and Take stall is where people in Deeside can take their unwanted goods and surplus. Organisers Frank and Vic set up the stall by scouring their own wardrobes, lofts and garages for good quality things they no longer needed, and then started a collection point at a local skip.

Here they have been handed things like hamster cages, music centres, electronic games, jigsaws, books, clothes all neatly ironed, fridges, beds, settees, cookers, televisions, fruit trees, tomato plants, bicycles, and even a deep sea diver's suit. These are all items that would normally be thrown in the skip. Goods are simply laid out on tables for people to take, and people come along and maybe take something, and sometimes leave a donation. This money can only be used to buy land or space, in order to expand and perpetuate Give and Take. The Well Health group want the support of people nationally to make possible a life not dependent on high wages and high levels of spending.

Part Two –
The case studies

Introduction

The following 12 case studies have been carefully chosen to reflect the breadth of interest there is in creating sustainable solutions for a green economy. From the high earning businessman Alan Knight to the volunteer animal rights campaigner Patrick Smith, all the case studies share one common aspiration – to work towards a greener future. We wanted each case study to represent a different industry – for example we have fashion designer Britta Boyer representing creative arts and design, and builder/architect Jenny Hall representing construction.

As far as possible, we have included all areas of the economy from transport to energy, from organic growing to development, and all types of work – self-employment, local and national government work, volunteering, employment with a business, working for a charity. Reading all the case studies gives you a good idea of the wide spectrum of green employment possibilities.

Each case study is backed up by the information you need to get on – educational requirements, contact details and career options. After reading the case studies, look in the directory to find the organisations, books and magazines that will help you find the work you want. The list below will help you find the case studies you are most interested in.

Snapshots of sustainability

Jenny Hall – Self-employed architect and builder.
Construction – page 76.
"Starting my NVQ as the only woman ever to have done the course wasn't fun. It didn't help being so much older – not interested in fast cars and TV. I just tolerated the lads until they were used to me being too stubborn to give in."

Jamie Saunders – Sustainability Co-ordinator (Policy), City of Bradford Metropolitan District Council.
Local authorities – page 78.
"This is pretty much what I've always wanted to do, though I do have the odd day of wishing to retire early and rest! I value the ability to be part of a wider change within the UK – and in local government in particular – in addressing sustainability and long-term solutions."

Steve Ward – Renewable energy engineer, Intermediate Technology Development Group.
Development – page 80.
"At the moment I am looking at ways of improving the energy efficiency of small pottery industries in India, and small sawmills in Ghana. My current salary is £20,500 per annum which is reasonable for this line of work. Given that I also have a very good working environment I certainly don't feel underpaid."

Helen Carver – Marketing manager, Energy Efficiency and Environmental Technology Best Practice Programmes.
Energy conservation and waste management – page 82.
"Thinking about it, I actually think I've been very lucky. I always wanted to link my geography and marketing skills with my environmental knowledge and conscience, and the job I have is an ideal job in which to do it."

Dr Alan Knight – Environmental Policy Controller, B&Q.
Environmental policy management – page 84.
"I have been Environmental Policy Controller of B&Q for 9 years. I chose this role because it allows me to challenge the paradigm that environment is anti-business. It is not – in fact, done well it is good business."

Sheila Clifford – Shop manager, Out of This World.
Retail – page 86.
"I worked for an insurance company for 14 years, then got to a stage in my life when I wanted to do something more worthwhile, but didn't have a clue what. Then I saw a programme about a new chain of ethical

supermarkets – one was in Bristol, my home town. I visited and was so impressed that I began volunteering on Saturdays. After five months a vacancy for an assistant manager came up."

Britta Boyer – Self-employed fashion designer.
Creative arts and design – page 88.
"I have always had a passion for fabrics, clothes and colour! My choice of sustainable design within the fashion industry means that I am working against the grain but this has encouraged me to find unusual solutions."

Wynn and Dale Garnes – Organic growers.
Organic growing – page 90.
"When the sun peeps out, when shoots and buds are bursting forth and when we open the polytunnel doors and are engulfed with the scents of a hundred and one herbs – it's the only place under heaven to be! What's important is that we're doing something we enjoy."

Dave Tobutt – Transport manager, Guildford Borough Council.
Transport – page 92.
"I was interested in mechanical engineering as a schoolboy, and my ambition has always been to be happy in what I do and be successful. My work means I can make a positive contribution to the environment by ensuring that the vehicles we purchase are designed to produce less pollutants."

Chris Laughton – Managing director, The Solar Design Company.
Renewable energy – page 94.
"I'm self-employed and run my own business. My job title varies! To other tradespeople I'm a heating engineer. To potential customers, I'm a solar and heating engineer. To unsolicited sales calls, I'm the managing director. To anyone else I'm a designer of solar energy systems."

David Blair – Woodsman, sole trader and director, Eco-op Ltd Workers Co-operative.
Ecological restoration and conservation – page 96.

"I've had many roles along the way – traveller, mechanic, engineering designer. I've established a craft shop, worked at house renovation, and at a willow nursery. But I followed my path with heart. I had no experience of woodland management when I came here – I'd never even felled a tree!"

Patrick Smith – Volunteer campaigner, Veggies Catering Campaign.
Campaigning and communication – page 98.
"A recent study put animal farming second only to private car use amongst the fundamental environmental problems facing the planet. Veggies actively campaigns against animal farming and promotes vegan living. We cater at festivals, green events and demonstrations, using no animal ingredients whatsoever."

A guide to the case studies

Why choose this career area?

These sections are intended as introductions and we encourage you to investigate further by getting hold of some of the many books available...

Key Contacts: These are the people who can help you get started. In most sections there is one environmental organisation and one general organisation, e.g. an institution which monitors the whole industry, not just the environmental sector.

Formal educational qualifications...are sometimes required, sometimes not. We have tried to indicate at what level – i.e. GCSE, A level, degree, postgraduate – qualifications are necessary or desirable. Sometimes there is a choice. For example, gardeners don't need formal qualifications but they are available. We tell you when this option exists but we don't make the choice for you. If you have any doubt about the best option – paper qualifications or none – get in touch with the key contacts. They will outline the pros and cons of both, but the choice is very much down to the individual.

Or, if you prefer, learn the skills in a different way, as we suggested in chapter three. There isn't always an 'or', and if there isn't one, we haven't written it in.

Case studies: Who? What they do...
Employment status: are they self-employed, a volunteer, employed, etc?
Qualifications: what have they got? Some of the case studies didn't think their educational qualifications were relevant to their job, hence there are some blanks under this heading.

The case studies want to give you a snapshot of their lives. How they came to work in the field, why they are doing it, what they love about it and what they don't. Here you will find out what their work entails and we hope this will give you a good insight into the job.

Case studies are never enough of course, and we would recommend you try and get some work experience if you like the sound of something. Our subjects wanted to relate their experiences to you because they know that working for the environment is a rewarding experience. We hope they will inspire and encourage you.

The case studies

Construction

Why ecological building?

Building accounts for a large percentage of Britain's total annual energy consumption. Ecological building is about choosing the right materials and using them in a design that makes the most of them. Getting these two elements right saves large amounts of energy and reduces environmental pollution. Some housing designs go one step beyond – they actually produce their own renewable energy.

Building

> **Key Contacts:** Construction Industry Training Board – for details of qualifications and training. Association of Environment Conscious Building – publishes a magazine and essential members directory.

Formal educational qualifications are not required but a wide range are available. More important though is a commitment to quality and accuracy. Apprenticeships and NVQs are both available.

Or... If you prefer, learn the skills yourself by renovating your own home, joining a self-build co-operative or volunteering for an organisation that specialises in ecological building.

Architecture

> **Key Contacts:** Royal Institute of British Architects – careers and training information. The Ecological Design Association – a good source of inspiration and information.

Qualification as an architect takes seven years; five years of degree level study and two years of practical experience. The University of East London and CAT are now offering a joint programme leading to an MSc in architecture: advanced environmental and energy studies.

We chose Jenny Hall as the subject for this case study because she has managed to combine the two main career routes – architecture and building. She combines her design knowledge with her practical skills to maximise the creativity in her work, to make it more interesting and to have greater control over her working life.

Case study: Jenny Hall, ecobuilder.
Employment status: Self-employed designer and carpenter.
Qualifications: Architecture degree and NVQ II in carpentry and joinery.

"I wanted to be an architect when I was nine. I'm not really sure why. I've always been space-sensitive. When I studied architecture I realised I didn't want to work in an office so I thought carefully about my likes and dislikes. I wanted to work outdoors and with other people so I started conservation work. This led to voluntary work maintaining rural buildings in Spain which in turn led to paid work. When I came back to the UK, I started an NVQ in carpentry and joinery.

"Starting my NVQ as the only woman ever to have done the course wasn't fun. It didn't help being so much older – not interested in fast cars and TV. I had one very good tutor who cut me a lot of slack and was very positive. I just tolerated the lads until they were used to me being too stubborn to give in. After my Level II, I stopped studying because I was getting real work and wanted to explore that.

"I contacted the Association of Environment Conscious Building (AECB). Realising the wealth of organisations nationwide, I contacted members from their directory. Calling first to introduce myself and then sending on my CV, I got a fair bit of interest. With good feedback from Cindy Harris at CAT and the offer of the use of a workshop by two architectural designers, I moved to Machynlleth and have worked on various projects since.

"Have I had any setbacks? Only when I did things without really thinking about their value to me – like taking a TEFL course after university because a friend was doing it and it seemed like a good idea. I discovered I didn't want to teach English, but I probably knew that anyway. I learnt much more about myself and my needs on a two month sailing trip, which I did about five years ago.

"I've been working on my practical skills ever since. The joy of developing these skills and gaining in confidence is very satisfying. It's very empowering to be able to build. Physical work means I'm fit and strong. There are negatives too. Building can be a series of boring jobs repeated over and over again. It's important to me that I take on design and drawing work as well. My ideal is to work on both the design and building of a project that is ecologically sound. It seems a sensible way to develop."

Working for a local authority

Why work for a local authority?

Local Agenda 21 (LA21) stems from the 1992 Earth Summit in Rio, where there was international agreement that sustainable development should be prioritised in the 21st century at national and local government levels. The UK Government has requested all local authorities to develop LA21 strategies by the end of 2000, and working in this growing area can contribute to the implementation of sustainability in your region.

Key Contacts: Local Government National Training Organisation (LGNTO). Or contact the Personnel Officer of individual counties, metropolitan counties and London boroughs. In Scotland, contact the Chief Executive of your local region.

Formal education is required: there are varying levels of responsibility within the sustainability departments of local councils, from administrative support through to head of department – qualifications needed will vary accordingly, from 3 or 4 GCSE passes to postgraduate diplomas. Local authorities are usually very willing to provide training: it may be possible to start at a relatively low entry level and gain qualifications and experience "in-house".

We have chosen to profile Jamie Saunders to illustrate that working for a mainstream organisation such as a local council can be just as rewarding as working in the alternative sector. For Jamie, the satisfaction lies in being able to promote effective social change "from the inside".

"My role allows me to work on the inside of an organisation and within the mainstream to support the integration of sustainable thinking and practice. It means I can encourage the 'bridge-building' and joint working required to implement people-focused solutions to the challenges of today and the future."

Case study: Jamie Saunders.
Employment status: full-time, permanent employee.
Qualifications: degree in environmental science and geography.

"I am the Sustainability Co-ordinator (Policy) for the City of Bradford Metropolitan District Council, working with the Strategic Support Division. It's a permanent, full-time position. I act as an advocate and co-ordinator of sustainable development both for Bradford Council itself and within Bradford District as a whole, advising and promoting sustainable solutions.

"My work seeks to integrate a concern for the future with social, economic and environmental considerations, to bring about lasting changes in the long-term quality of life within the Bradford District. It also encourages organisations to recognise that social and environmental issues can be as significant as economic considerations when it comes to the 'bottom line'. I've been doing this kind of work for 7½ years, since 1992, when I was first employed as Environmental Audit Officer and then as Local Agenda 21 Co-ordinator. I work 37 hours per week plus evenings and weekends as required (flexitime and time in lieu are in operation), and my income is that of a senior policy officer within the public sector.

"How did I get to where I am today? After my degree I discovered permaculture. This helped me realise that people and organisations need solutions-based approaches to environmental issues. They should also be encouraged to explore the cultural, theoretical and practical aspects of sustainable development. To enhance my ability to promote this, I'm currently studying for a Masters Degree in Foresight and Future Studies at Leeds Metropolitan University (a 2-year, part-time course).

"One setback I've experienced is the lack of widespread understanding of sustainability. The breadth and complexity of my work can seem a bit of a drawback – and lead to information overload! Then there's the juggling act of balancing work, play and personal/home life. But this is pretty much what I've always wanted to do, though I do have the odd day of wishing to retire early and rest! I value the ability to be part of wider change within the UK – and local government in particular – in addressing sustainability and long-term solutions."

Development

Why development?

Sharing technological information will be an important part of the process of creating global sustainability. This is a two way process - with both developing and developed countries learning from each other. Development workers can bridge the gap between the two worlds - bringing knowledge in to the first world as well as taking it out.

Key Contacts: Intermediate Technology Development Group, Voluntary Services Overseas (VSO), United Nations Association International Service (UNAIS).

Formal educational qualifications are important. Our case study Steve Ward took an engineering degree with a strong emphasis on development. However, it is still possible to work in development if you have a standard technical training and a proven work record. VSO finds overseas placements for people from many different professions.

Gaining overseas voluntary work experience helps show potential employers that you have what it takes to occupy a paid position but organisations such as VSO do take people on on the basis of their skills used in non-development work. The Engineering Design and Appropriate Technology degree (EDAT) at Warwick University includes a placement overseas and various practical work projects.

We have chosen Steve Ward as our case study because he works specifically to increase the use of environmental technologies in developing countries. His experience also illustrates the advantages of backing up educational qualifications with voluntary work experience.

Case study: Steve Ward.

Employment status: Energy Projects Manager, Intermediate Technology Consultants.

Qualifications: degree in engineering design and appropriate technology (EDAT).

"I work for the consultancy arm of a UK national charity which aims to assist small producers in developing countries to achieve sustainable livelihoods through the use of appropriate technologies. I help regions and authorities to create renewable energy strategies, carry out policy research and prepare training materials for policy makers. At the moment I am looking at ways of improving the energy efficiency of small pottery industries in India and of small sawmills in Ghana. My current salary is £20,500 which is reasonable for this line of work. Given that I also have a very good working environment I certainly don't feel underpaid.

"I decided to study engineering when I was 18. It was either this, or do history! In the end I thought it was important to me to have a trade, and that if I was going to study something for 3 years at uni', then I wanted it to be something practical that I would use afterwards. There were also other driving influences. I wanted to travel the world and being an engineer seemed a good way to do this. Also my dad was an engineer (toolmaker) and I somehow wanted to continue the tradition! Mind you, I didn't want to just be an engineer designing bits for cars – I wanted to do something that I felt would be useful to society, which is why I went for the developing countries/renewables angle.

"The course I eventually chose was at Warwick University. The engineering design and appropriate technology degree was the only engineering course that appealed to me in 1990 as it specialised in technologies for developing countries and renewable energy. This was at heart a basic three year mechanical engineering degree, which gave me all the theoretical knowledge, and to a lesser extent, practical knowledge I would need to get a job as a professional engineer. However, the course also gave me some practical experience of working with renewable energy systems. I took a year out before my final year to work at a technology centre in Botswana. This experience of working overseas has proved invaluable with employers ever since, and was a fantastic personal experience.

"The next important career step was a 6 month volunteer placement at CAT. Here I assisted the site engineers in day-to-day maintenance as well as doing some work on new projects. I gained invaluable practical experience and took many of CAT's tremendously useful three day courses. By being very proactive and persistent, I was able to get a paid trainee position at a nearby renewable energy company called Dulas Ltd. At the end of the six months, I was taken on as a full-time engineer in the hydro department. After two years there I left to pursue other interests before returning to engineering at ITC.

"Although there is too much paperwork in my present job and I don't get to get my hands dirty much, the positives outweigh these small negatives. I can travel to interesting places, influence policy makers like the World Bank and EC, work at the cutting edge of renewable energy projects and meet with colleagues from all over the world. I also enjoy a good working atmosphere and team spirit. This is very important."

Energy conservation and waste minimisation

Why energy conservation?

"Waste minimisation and energy conservation is all about getting more from less." This is the message of the conservationists, and they have a strong point. Conservationists aim to get more from less, increasing standards of living, productivity and efficiency, and cutting pollution. They are true pioneers - practical, positive and penny-pinching.

Key Contacts: Association for the Conservation of Energy (ACE), National Energy Foundation (NEF).

Formal educational requirements vary. There are a wide number of jobs in this industry – conservation assessor, installer, researcher, advisor, local authority energy officer, engineer; educational requirements are different for each one.

Conservation assessors go through a formal training procedure organised by ACE and NEF. Installers need basic training, either from a local Energy Advice Centre or through ACE and NEF. A researcher developing new products will have a specialist qualification (normally a degree) in a relevant subject like engineering. A local authority energy officer will meet normal council requirements for a management level position (see case studies on Dave Tobutt and Jamie Saunders). An engineer designing waste management systems will normally have a relevant degree.

We chose Helen Carver as our case study because her job involves both of the main areas of activity – energy conservation and waste minimisation. As a marketing manager for the Government's Environmental Technology Best Practice Programme, she encourages companies to change their production practices by showing them how other companies have done the same and made huge savings.

Case study: Helen Carver.

Employment status: marketing manager – Energy Efficiency and Environment Technology Best Practice Programme. Employed by national government.

Qualifications: BSc in geography/MSc in marketing.

"I help UK companies, large and small, to cost-effectively reduce their raw material, water and energy consumption. This helps reduce CO_2 and other greenhouse gas emissions as well as saving the earth's valuable water and raw material resources.

"I do this by taking examples of good practice and promoting them to the rest of the industry; companies see how energy conservation has benefitted others and how it can benefit them. In particular, I have designed, implemented and managed the strategic marketing and promotional activities of the volatile organic chemical, metal finishing, printing, ceramic, glass, mineral and paper portfolios.

"How did I get to where I am today? I did a geography first degree and then a marketing MSc. Then I started work for AEA Technology in 1993 as a technical manager for the wind section in the Government's New and Renewable Energy Programme. At the end of 1994, I transferred within the same company to the marketing department and my present job. Prior to 1993 I did different holiday and summer jobs (selling on a stand, working in a bank, nanny and garage assistant). I also took a pre-university year off and did lots of travelling, working my way around the world.

"Thinking about it, I actually think I've been very lucky. I always wanted to link my geography and marketing skills with my environmental knowledge and conscience, and the job I have is an ideal job in which to do it. I also don't think I've had many setbacks in getting the job I have now. On a personal level I am dyslexic and so have had to cope with that; to help me succeed with my dyslexia I have a very supportive family and, quietly, I am a very determined person.

"Helping companies to save money and help the environment at the same time is very rewarding. This is especially so when you see that a company has made a big saving through implementing a low-cost measure (waste minimisation action). That gives you a good feeling. I also like meeting people from a very wide range of companies – from small, independent dry-cleaners to the ICIs of this world. I get a chance to visit different industry factories and I start to learn about their processes and operations which is all very interesting. I also talk to influential people such as trade associations, local business groups and governments about how we can encourage companies to take up energy conservation and waste minimisation. On the down side, as with most jobs, there is lots of paperwork and form filling! Also, things can move very slowly because changes have to be approved by the Government."

Environmental policy management

Why environmental policy management?

Every business, whether big or small, causes some environmental impact. The size of this ecological 'footprint' will vary according to the firm's practices. More and more companies are striving to improve their performance in this area, by using assessment techniques such as green audits to identify where change is needed. Working to create appropriate policies can be a valuable way of reducing environmental damage.

> **Key Contacts:** almost every national company now has some form of environmental policy. For specific vacancies contact the relevant head office and ask for their personnel department. Also see p.137.

Formal educational qualifications are required. This is an area where relevant qualifications will almost certainly be needed. For managerial level positions, you will need a degree or postgraduate qualification. As a joint degree in sustainability and business management may not be available, a degree in one discipline followed by postgraduate study of the other is a potential alternative. Contact UCAS for available courses.

Public sector training and experience is valuable in this field, so a shift from a similar level of responsibility in local government could be a possibility. Consider working for a company or institution that is renowned for its work in sustainability and is invited to provide consultancy to industry or business.

We chose Alan Knight as our case study because he has the opportunity to influence people and organisations worldwide. He and the team he has gathered have been responsible for dramatic improvements in DIY retailer B&Q's environmental performance, and are constantly working to further their achievements. In 1998, Dr Knight was awarded the OBE for "services to environment and business".

Case study: Alan Knight.
Employment status: Full-time, permanent employee - B&Q.
Qualifications: PhD in marine biology.

"I have been Environmental Policy Controller at B&Q for 9 years. I chose this role because it allows me to challenge the paradigm that environment is anti-business. It is not – in fact, done well – it is good business. My remit is to ensure that B&Q is at the cutting edge of social, ethical and environmental issues, and, of course, that through this it is maximising commercial benefit. In my work, I'm in a position to inspire people with power – buyers, non-governmental organisations (NGOs) and our supply chains – to recognise the importance of social and environmental issues.

"Environmental concerns arise because we don't appreciate enough that we all live in one neighbourhood – the planet. I work to ensure that B&Q is a good trading neighbour. Suppliers of all the products we sell are graded on their environmental awareness and performance, in terms of policy and action. We place real emphasis on any products sourced from developing countries or from woods. We have special projects in India, the Philippines and China, dramatically improving working conditions. Closer to home, our stores promote and take part in recycling schemes, energy efficiency and local community work.

"My work involves running a think tank that recommends policy on all environmental, ethical and sustainable development issues affecting B&Q's operations and product range. I am also responsible for helping the rest of the Kingfisher Group (of which B&Q is part) to adopt similar approaches. In a typical year, I will have meetings with royalty, government ministers, and organisations like the World Bank or the UN. I sit on many committees, including the World Wildlife Fund International Futures Group. I work 60 hours a week, but, though career progression from here is limited, I enjoy everything about my job – I achieve things, travel the world – it's interesting, worthwhile and fun! I earn £60,000 per year. The major difficulty I've experienced has been the poor quality of NGOs' respect for business and profit, but I've overcome this although I am proud to have no formal training in sustainable development. Academics over-intellectualise the topic. It is commonsense. Sustainability has to take into account the profitability of both the planet and its people. It is perhaps best defined as 'improving our quality of life in a way which helps our local and global neighbours improve theirs, without compromising the ability of future generations to do the same.'

"This type of work has always been my ambition. After my PhD in marine biology I spent a year as a marine biologist, then 8 months at Hamleys and 8 months as a consultant. Then I saw this job advertised – and got it!"

Retail

Why retail?

With people becoming more aware of the social and environmental impact of their spending patterns, consumer power is an increasingly important issue. Sourcing and selling fairly traded, local and organic produce provides a valuable service, offering busy shoppers an easy way to reduce their households' environmental footprints.

> **Key Contacts:** to work for a local shop – apply within! For national chain stores, e.g. Out Of This World, Body Shop, Realfoods, Oxfam and other charities, contact their head offices.

Formal educational requirements vary depending on the shop and the level of responsibility the job carries. For traditional shop work, junior trainees or trainee supervisors need 3–4 GCSEs or equivalent; trainee managers and buyers, 2 A levels or even a degree. There are also BTEC and SCOTVEC (see SQA) courses available in retailing. Part-time, weekend or voluntary work will count as valuable experience.

Or... With enough capital (perhaps from a business loan – see your bank's small business advisor) you could set up your own shop. Or you could consider making goods (perhaps from recycled materials) to sell in local or national shops. Always get advice on this and consider your potential market and set-up costs very carefully indeed. It will probably be at least a couple of years before you are making a profit.

We chose Sheila Clifford as a case study for two reasons. Firstly, her profile shows how satisfying retail work can be when you're selling products you really believe in. Secondly, Sheila provides a great example to those who feel they're stuck in the wrong career - it's worth gathering the courage to start again, as her story shows.

Case study:	Sheila Clifford.
Employment status:	Shop manager, Out of This World; full-time, permanent employee of members' co-operative.

"All Out Of This World supermarkets have a principle of environmental sustainability. The store I manage has a café and fair trade craft section, in addition to a wide range of food products. I order stock, do paperwork, organise staffing levels, serve customers, and stock shelves. I have great fun finding new products, especially the gifts. My starting salary is £15,000 per annum – less than my old job, but I'm not doing this for the money!

"I'm paid for 40 hours, but being a perfectionist, and fairly new to retail, I put in more, partly because I love what I do! There are minor catastrophes – the freezer defrosting, or the burglar alarm going off – but they're soon sorted. I've been in retail for 2 years. I worked for an insurance company for 14 years, then got to a stage in my life when I wanted to do something more worthwhile, but didn't have a clue what. Then I saw a programme about a new chain of ethical supermarkets – one was in Bristol, my home town. I visited, and was so impressed that I began volunteering on Saturdays, whilst still doing my 'normal' job and living in Wales!

"After 5 months, a vacancy for an assistant manager came up. I had very little retail experience and didn't think I stood much of a chance. I think my enthusiasm got me through the interview! Accepting the job meant my partner Ray and I selling our house and moving. Then the Bristol shop closed. This was a very sad time – we had a great team, but alternative premises couldn't be found, so I could have been out of work after only 9 months!

"However, I was offered an assistant manager's post in the Newcastle shop – 300 miles from home. But we both felt strongly that I'd made the right career decision, we both support the ideas behind Out Of This World, and we love organic food – the job suited our lifestyle. So, off to Newcastle! 5 months later, we were on the move again. There was a vacancy in the Cheltenham branch – a shop with a café – and closer to home! After four months, the manager left, and I was promoted. So in two years I've gone from volunteer to manager. Lots of hard work, a few tears of frustration on the way, and some sleepless nights, but also lots of laughs and a great sense of achievement, especially when I help a customer find exactly what they want."

Creative arts...design and manufacture

Why creative arts?

Creative artists such as fashion designers, potters, chair makers or product designers can make or break the ecological value of an item not only by choosing the right materials but by making its manufacture energy efficient and economical. In the creative arts the message is just as important as the medium, and writers and those working in the visual arts have the power to make a point – be it in a campaign, news article or art gallery.

> **Key Contacts:** Ecological Design Association (EDA) – for magazine and register; Design Council – for information about training and qualifications. For fashion design: Textile Environment Network – for environmental information; CAPITB Trust – for general careers information.

Formal educational requirements vary. This is such a broad area of work that there is no standard route, although many people working in what we loosely describe as the creative industries have undergone some sort of degree level education. As the level of training differs from job to job, it is best to refer to a book like Kogan Page's *The A-Z of Careers and Jobs* for good information about educational requirements. Alternatively visit your local careers service.

Or... Learn your trade through short courses and practice. For example, woodland crafts (e.g. the making of furniture and tools from coppice wood) can be learned in this way. You may even find someone who can take you on as an apprentice. Read *Permaculture* magazine for course details.

We chose Britta Boyer as our case study because she is tackling an unsustainable industry from within, while creating imaginative designs which are attractive in their own right, not just because they are environmentally sensitive. Britta is currently working for a manufacturing company while she seeks finance for her own ecolabel, earth 33.

Case study: Britta Boyer.
Employment status: Self-employed fashion designer.
Qualifications: BA Hons in fashion print, HND in fashion design and technology.

"I have always had a passion for fabrics, clothes and colour! I would say that I respond well to visual stimulus and aesthetics. This probably comes from my nomadic lifestyle and colourful upbringing – living in various parts of the globe. I knew from a very early age I wanted to be a fashion designer. The environmental aspect came later when I realised how fickle and wasteful the fashion industry was. I almost gave up my career after completing my degree course and then realised that I may be able to do something positive to change things rather than shun the whole industry.

"So I started a fashion label committed to sustainable design in the fashion industry. The label is earth 33 and it specialises in the use of environmentally conscious fabrics. My choice of sustainable design within the industry means that I am working against the grain, but this has encouraged me to find unusual solutions. I would like to think that I am doing something positive, appealing to customer taste and style as well as offering an alternative to those who take environmental issues seriously.

"As a sole trader, I have had to work very hard – anywhere between 40 and 80 hours a week. I do the bookkeeping, administration (paying bills and answering the phone!), sales, PR, organising production, delivering collections on time to retailers, and I spend a limited amount of time designing and planning future collections. I would advise anyone who does the same to expect very little income for at least two years – if not longer.

"I have had to work in other jobs to support myself. I have read and heard from other businesses that you do not start seeing a return for about five years and after the seventh you have the potential to make a good profit and a healthy income. In this time I have had to live a minimalist lifestyle. I do not regret this but it can get me down, as does the loneliness of running your own business.

"It has been a long journey and I have worked very hard. Have I had any setbacks? Yes, a few! Half of my first collection was stolen in transit to a trade show. I was not insured, therefore lost money and had to virtually start again. Another time, a few weeks prior to the first of the 1998 London shows, my main supplier went into liquidation, which meant I was unable to take any orders, as the cloth (recycled denim) was no longer available.

"With the support of my family – my stepfather financed my next collection – I overcame these setbacks because I maintained a strong sense of belief in my goal. The best thing about my job is when people respond positively to the environmental ethos which earth 33 aims to maintain, as well as appreciating the simplicity of the designs. It is people, after all, who buy into the idea and allow the business to grow."

Organic growing

Why organic growing?

The market for organic food has risen dramatically in the last few years. This is because consumers know what they are getting when they buy organic – tasty food, grown without chemicals. Two three-letter acronyms – BSE and GMO – have done more for organics than years of campaigning. Organic growing is a viable alternative which guarantees safe food without harming the environment.

> **Key Contacts:** the main two are the Soil Association for farmers, and the HDRA for gardeners. However, there are many different systems for organic growing that are worth following up. Try the following organisations for further information: the Permaculture Association for whole organic systems; VOHAN (Vegan Organic Network) for vegan organic growing; the Bio-dynamic Agricultural Association for a spiritual slant on horticulture; Plants for a Future for perennial planting; and Thrive (Horticultural Therapy), an association that works with the disabled.

Formal educational qualifications are not required for careers in organic growing, but are available – including HNDs and degrees in both organic farming and gardening. Some employers prefer applicants with formal qualifications but experience is just as important.

Or... Learn the skills by volunteering through WWOOF (Willing Workers on Organic Farms), by working for an organic grower or by using your own garden or allotment as a training ground.

We have chosen Wynn and Dale Garnes as our case studies because they reflect many of the values most commonly found in organic growers – dedication, enthusiasm and gritty determination. They also show that you don't need a large amount of land to practice organic growing.

Case study: Wynn and Dale Garnes.
Employment status: partners in their own business, Blooming Things (an organic plant nursery).

"Plants can help reduce global warming by converting harmful CO_2 into oxygen. Our own small enterprise may seem insignificant compared with the destruction of a rainforest, but if we do our bit and encourage others to do a bit as well, together we will have more impact.

"We've been doing this work for 10 years now and we have to do everything for the business – administration, production, marketing, packing, growing, maintenance...the list could go on. It seems like we work 200 hours a week, but it's probably in the region of 70, though even that can sometimes match our blood pressure and rise enormously! Ultimately the buck stops with us and off duty time is restricted – plants can't help themselves to a drink or get up to close the door if there's a bit of a draught.

"How much money do we hope to make? The actual figure is irrelevant. We didn't set out to make megabucks – just to provide ourselves with a living. When we started, we really only wanted to achieve a high level of self-sufficiency, with paid employment being an option rather than a necessity. When we decided to generate an income, we narrowed our options down to something that we could do together; Blooming Things is the result. Actually the pay is abysmal, but this work is not the thing to do if 'reward' for you means the bankable stuff.

"Has this always been our ambition? No. We've both been involved in quite a wide range of occupations. Each of us served in the Royal Air Force, and before and after our time there we've passed through dental nursing, electrical/electronic engineering, clerking, physical training instructing, selling furniture, teaching, lecturing and undoubtedly the best training ground of all, parenthood! Each of these jobs, especially our time in the RAF, and extra-especially the zillion years we've been around doing all these things, has left us with insight, practical experience and adaptability – assets which may not always bring about the quick fix but which always stand us in good stead, especially on those freezing, wet, windy January mornings when we find ourselves slithering around, ankle-deep in mud and frozen to the marrow. Besides, we know that when the sun peeps out, when shoots and buds are bursting forth and when we open the polytunnel doors and are engulfed by the scents of a hundred and one herbs – it's the only place under heaven to be!

"What's important is that we're doing something we enjoy. It's positive, creative, requires mental and physical skills and, because of the variety and differing levels of tasks involved, it is never boring, and bearing in mind the difficulties expressed earlier, it's a challenge."

Transport

Why transport management?

Fumes from vehicles cause many environmental problems: burning fossil fuels releases greenhouse gases, creates smog, and damages our health, contributing to various respiratory complaints. Traffic also causes noise pollution and demands road building, often at great ecological cost. Transport managers can significantly reduce the impact of their vehicles by pursuing enlightened policies, using the least damaging fuels, and testing and implementing "cleaner" quieter technologies.

> **Key Contacts:** Local Government National Training Organisation (LGNTO). Or contact the Personnel Officer of individual counties, metropolitan counties and London boroughs. In Scotland, contact the Chief Executive of Scottish regions.

Formal educational requirements vary according to level of entry, though GCSE passes are probably the bare minimum, and some positions will even require postgraduate qualifications. NVQs are also increasingly being recognised.

Or... You may be able to transfer skills gained in transport divisions in the private sector. You could also seek work in the private sector and attempt to change attitudes from within. All supermarkets and companies with national delivery networks (e.g. mail order catalogues, car part manufacturers) need to maximise efficiency, making sure that deliveries and collections are appropriately routed, and to minimise pollution levels. Contact the personnel officer at the head office of the relevant company.

We chose Dave Tobutt as our case study because he works constantly to achieve lower emission and noise levels, and is always looking for new, viable fuel sources. At one stage, he ran trials with an electric car. Though, sadly, that particular model was not suitable for council use, there are all kinds of possibilities for alternative fuel sources for vehicles and machinery in the future.

Case study: Dave Tobutt.
Employment status: Transport manager, Guildford Borough Council. Full-time, permanent employee.

"I was interested in mechanical engineering as a schoolboy, and my ambition has always been to be happy in what I do and be successful. My work means that I can make a positive contribution to the environment by ensuring that the vehicles we purchase are designed to produce less pollutants, and are quieter in operation. I am also in a position to explore the use of alternative fuels.

"I am responsible for purchasing all vehicles and plant for the authority, ranging from a huge refuse freighter to minibuses for transporting the disabled, to small grass-cutting machines. I ensure drivers and operators receive training on correct and safe use, that everything is maintained correctly and legally, and that our repair workshops operate cost-effectively. I am also responsible for MOT testing, the authority's Goods Vehicles Operating Licence, and the supply of all fuels.

"One example of environmental benefit that I've achieved is by changing our diesel to Ultra Low Sulphur Diesel. This, coupled with the latest exhaust technology, has enabled us to achieve emission levels on a par with a gas-powered engine. We are also conducting trials using liquid petroleum gas (LPG) and compressed natural gas; if gas propulsion is viable, I will expand the programme. I am always looking for new developments that will allow us to lower emission levels without lowering standards of service. Hydrogen propulsion could be a possibility for future trials.

"Another area of my work involves giving lectures to all council staff on defensive driving techniques (the art of driving to avoid preventable accidents). This is perhaps the most satisfying part of my role: seeing vehicles and plant operated in a safe and efficient way. On the negative side: it saddens me that not enough resources are available to train young people for the future.

"I am scheduled to work a 37 hour week though it normally reaches 50 hours. But the post holds a high level of responsibility, and my salary reflects this.

"I have worked within the transport industry for 35 years, with various employers, and have had many setbacks in my career, such as being made redundant and being unsuccessful with job applications. But I got to where I am today because I always believed in my own ability to succeed. Of course, I put in a lot of commitment and effort, too. I started as a trainee in the workshops and worked my way through the grades, becoming foreman, fleet inspector, training officer, transport supervisor and finally transport manager."

Renewable energy...engineer and advisor

Why renewable energy?

This is one of the fastest growing sectors of the energy market – a trend strengthened by the involvement of, amongst others, large oil producers Shell and BP. Not only are current stocks of fossil fuels running out, burning them is also extremely bad for the environment. We all use energy but there are alternatives to fossil fuels which don't harm the environment, including solar, wind, hydro, wave, tidal, geothermal and biofuel.

Key Contacts: CAT – for contacts, publications and courses; the Engineering Council – for general careers advice.

Formal educational qualifications are usually required – degrees being the norm and a postgraduate qualification giving you the edge. Specialist degrees are the best but are in short supply. A straight engineering degree will teach you the nuts and bolts. In association with CAT, Liverpool John Moores University is now running the first BSc in sustainable technology.

Or... Build your skills through volunteering, practice and basic paid engineering work. It is not unknown for people to work as engineers without degrees but it is less common. If you are considering working as a development engineer in the Third World, see case study Steve Ward (page 80) or contact the Intermediate Technology Development Group (page 123).

If you already have the skills, find out how to apply them in an ecological way. To find out more about renewable energy, visit CAT's website, www.cat.org.uk or phone 01654 702400 for book and courses information.

We chose to feature Chris Laughton because his example clearly illustrates the varied roles and responsibilities you have to take on when you run your own business. Chris also emphasises the long hours involved – he often works 12 hour days, especially in summer. But the rewards are there too, as he explains.

Case study: Chris Laughton.
Employment status: Self-employed manager/director of own business,
The Solar Design Company

"I chose my occupation because it offers positive solutions to environmental issues, involving creative manual work, modest travel opportunities, interaction with interesting and vibrant people – all within a growing economic market. It benefits the environment by reducing fossil fuel dependency. I provide equipment enabling efficiency, energy conservation and access to renewables, particularly solar.

"I'm self-employed and run my own business, The Solar Design Company. My job title varies! To other tradespeople I'm a heating engineer. To potential customers I'm a solar and heating engineer. To unsolicited sales calls I'm the managing director. To anyone else I'm a designer of solar energy systems.

"What does the work entail? For about 4 days a week, it's finding potential customers, visiting prospective projects, preparing design and costs, organising tools, materials and workers, on site construction, and paperwork. Roughly one more day is spent on technical data, storage and stocking of materials, creating artwork, finance forecasting, tool/vehicle maintenance, scouring trade journals/the Internet, computer upgrades/training, and paperwork. Occasional work includes presentations, media work, and photographs and paperwork. Oh, did I mention the endless paperwork? Actually it's mostly done on the computer but it's still very tedious.

"I'm not sure how many hours a week I work – I've never added them up. Probably most waking hours, especially if thinking time is considered as working. On site, it's never less than a 12-hour day. Income? I'm happy if it's more than £10,000 net profit in a year, not that I really know. It's something the accountants tell me after about a year's delay.

"This type of work has been my ambition since my late 20s – I've been doing it for six years now. I went from school to university, then spent 10 years in various occupations, accumulating tools and skills along the way. In particular, I picked up plumbing, electrical and roofing abilities, often volunteering or odd-jobbing. Then a major solar manufacturing company ran a free training day which helped crystallise all I'd learnt. My environmental convictions came from a year with Greenpeace USA, where I also discovered the importance of communicating enthusiasm. My interest in conventional heating and ventilating came from a year as a small business energy advisor.

"Setbacks along the way include wasted time applying for funding that never materialised, and getting a large fine for inadvertently passing the VAT threshold. I also had to overcome a lack of initial finance by saving hard from small jobs.

"The best things about my job are the freedom and flexibility. The worst thing? The paperwork!"

Ecological restoration and conservation

Why ecological restoration?

Worldwide, natural habitat and wilderness are disappearing fast. Deforestation is a serious global concern. However, we will continue to need products from our woodlands, and proper management of these resources is the only way to ensure a sustainable supply. One way to achieve this is to encourage natural regeneration of native species, coupled with selective harvesting methods.

Key Contacts: Trees for Life, The Countryside Agency, Countryside Council for Wales, The Forestry Commission, Lantra, Plants For A Future.

Formal educational qualifications are not as important as practical skills learned on the job, but, having said this, various courses are available in countryside management, forestry, etc. from NVQ to postgraduate level. Managerial roles may require a degree.

Or... This is an area where voluntary experience is highly regarded and can often lead to paid work. Contact BTCV, The Association of National Parks and Countryside Voluntary Wardens (ANPCVW), and your local Woodland Trust. If you can raise the capital, either as an individual or as part of a co-operative, you could consider buying a piece of woodland and implementing your own management plan. Depending on your aims, it could be run, for instance, as an educational resource or to sell woodland products.

Our profile of David Blair illustrates that when you have a passion for the work you are doing – however hard that work may be – you will still find it intensely fulfilling. Though the financial rewards of his lifestyle are limited, David finds that the beauty of his surroundings and the relative freedom to dictate his working schedule more than compensate.

Case study:	David Blair.
Employment status:	Self-employed and member of worker co-operative.
Qualifications:	BSc in mechanical engineering; Permaculture design course graduate; chainsaw licence holder.

"My main work is ecological restoration, managing 30 acres of ancient semi-natural oak woodland. It is one of the most diverse ecosystems in Europe, but mixed conifer, underplanted in 1963, is slowly extinguishing the native woodland, and some areas are infested with rhododendron. I remove the exotics (non-native species) to encourage natural regeneration.

"Besides being a woodsman and managing the Dun Beag project, I run an ecological business – Ecobiz – as a sole trader. I am also the director and secretary of Eco-op Ltd Worker Co-operative, and manager of Dun Beag community composting scheme. I aim to apply the principles of Permaculture to all my work, including our forest gardens, mushroom cultivation, and polytunnels.

"I have never really drawn an income. I use what I need to live – very little, as I live in the wood with no mains services. However, I expect to live well (within my means), and I'm installing a renewable energy system – so, finally, I should have electricity this winter.

"I work in a beautiful place, I believe in what I do, I (mostly) choose the agenda, it's creative and it gives me freedom. It's hard graft but I love it – the only bad things about it really are the risk of injury and people misunderstanding what I do. I guess I work a lot of hours in the week all in all, but the work is so diverse and variable it doesn't seem too bad. There is so much work that I employ my brother Robert for 3 days a week.

"The felling is not always easy, as some trees need to be winched down. The thinnest are used for fencing materials, the next size up as furniture or firewood, and the biggest are 'slabbed' into planks, which are dried in a solar timber-seasoning tunnel, then hand-crafted into chunky furniture. Offcuts become firewood, and brash is stacked as habitat or stock barriers. The pigs, Chong and Pong, then prepare the ground for natural regeneration!

"I've had many roles along the way – traveller, mechanic, engineering designer. I've established a craft shop, worked at house renovation, and at a willow nursery. But I followed my path with heart. I had no experience of woodland management when I came here – I'd never even felled a tree!

"It hasn't been that easy, though. Setbacks have included difficulties with planning authorities, misunderstandings with neighbours (including my pigs eating their gardens), deer, rabbits and slugs eating my fruit trees – even drought killing the mushrooms – in Argyll!

"This hasn't always been my ambition, but I wouldn't be disappointed if it had, 'cause I love it!"

Campaigning and communication

Why campaigning?

Raising public awareness of an issue is a crucial step in effecting change; for example Greenpeace and Friends of the Earth have played a vital role in changing environmental legislation. A whole spectrum of organisations, from international charities to local action groups, is crying out for volunteers in almost every sphere of work, from lending a hand or a sympathetic ear, to co-ordinating media campaigns.

Key Contacts: The National Council for Voluntary Opportunities (NCVO). The Charity Commission can provide a list of registered charities - some of whom may have paid opportunities, too. Wednesday's *Guardian* lists charity appointments, from voluntary work to senior positions such as the managing director of an international charity. Try also the National Union of Journalists. If you are specifically interested in animal welfare, or promoting a vegan or vegetarian lifestyle, key contacts are BUAV, the Vegan Society and Animal Aid. You might also consider looking for work in a local health food shop or restaurant – just ask at the counter if they know of any vacancies, or advertise on their noticeboard.

Formal educational qualifications are not always necessary, but often help to develop essential communication skills. For paid positions qualification requirements vary according to role and responsibility (for example a media/journalism diploma or degree may be needed for work in a national organisation's PR office). Whatever the job, it's safe to say that voluntary experience will always be a valuable addition to your CV.

Or... A particular issue may inspire you to start your own action group. Be aware that this will almost certainly involve long hours and a punishing phone bill. Get in touch with others working for similar causes, for mutual support. The Internet is a great way to do this, but also put adverts in local shops or cafes where like-minded people will spot them.

Patrick Smith's case study shows how, for some people, financial reward is irrelevant compared to the satisfaction of dedicating their life to a cause that's important to them. Over the years, Patrick has sometimes been paid for his work, though currently he is volunteering. What's vital to him is the knowledge that he is spreading the vegan message, and promoting animal rights.

Case study: Patrick Smith.
Employment status: Volunteer worker and campaigner.

"I'm a founder member and part-time worker with Veggies Catering Campaign, in Nottingham. We cater at festivals, green events and demonstrations, using no animal ingredients whatsoever. We also run a daily food stall in Nottingham city centre and manufacture frozen vegan 'sosages' and burgers. I also compile the *Animal Contacts Directory*. How does my work benefit the environment? A recent study put animal farming second only to private car use amongst the fundamental environmental problems facing the planet. It contributes to pollution, land and water wastage, energy use, deforestation, and so on. Veggies actively campaigns against animal farming and promotes vegan living. We minimise vehicle use, recycle just about everything and fund Nottingham's Rainbow Centre, providing resources for many local campaigning groups and individuals.

"I've worked here for fifteen years, ever since Veggies was founded – sometimes as a volunteer, sometimes paid. Currently, I'm technically an unemployed volunteer animal rights campaigner, so the amount of hours I work per week varies greatly, depending on jobseeking commitments, the time of year and on the input of other volunteers.

"What sort of income do I get? None! For me, the worst thing about my job is the fact that our work, which has so many benefits, isn't officially recognised or endorsed by the Government. But I chose this type of work because it offers me the opportunity to really make a difference and change opinions – our work performs an important educational role, whilst every meal served is one less slice off a cow. As well as informing about the benefits of veganism, we offer solutions to the problems. This particular role wasn't always my ambition, but now I can't imagine doing anything more rewarding.

"I've had a few other jobs along the way. It was while I was a Student Union Officer that I developed an interest in community-related work. Later, I became a manager for a national pizza chain. During the time I was working there, I became vegetarian, so I was reluctant to promote meat-based meals. On moving to manage a Nottingham branch, I called the local Vegetarian Society contact and animal rights group, and met the founders of Veggies. The rest is history!

"We've had a few setbacks – the rain and mud at Glastonbury; trashed vehicles; a stolen trailer and an ex-volunteer ripping off several hundred pounds. Key co-workers have dropped out or moved on. Our recent fifteenth birthday party was invaded by the police! The worst setback was the takeover of our major ingredients supplier by Unilever, a massive multinational we don't want to support. We changed supplier, but our sales dropped dramatically. Through all of this, the crew have rallied together and pitched in. We always surge on through times of hardship."

What advice do you have for readers of this book?

Jenny Hall

"What advice do I have for readers of this book? Ask yourself what is it you'd really like and make small steps to achieve that. By constantly adjusting your needs and wants, all that you do will be a part of your process. Take other people's advice when it fits, but be wary of leading anyone's life other than your own. I have found voluntary work a very useful way of learning and have been on Income Support and very low wages doing what's been important to me. You can live real cheap if need be. Be true to yourself."

Dave Tobutt

"Whatever career path you decide on, always give 100 per cent in effort and enthusiasm – be prepared for setbacks – these will make you more determined to succeed."

"Determination and really knowing what you want to do. Once you know what you want to do, find out who does it and how you can be involved. If you can't get in one way, think laterally, can you get in another?

Helen Carver

"Often the dilemma is 'should I get work experience or a qualification to help me get that important first job?' When I wanted to get into marketing I asked many different marketing managers whether they wanted experience (e.g. in sales) or a marketing qualification first. Half said experience and the other half said the qualification. However, one person said that qualification might not help me get the first job but will help me to get promotions and further my career later on. After six years of marketing, I still think that was sound advice.

"There is no doubt that having the right qualifications and having done a few extra things (like travelling and working abroad) has helped me to stand out a little from the crowd and to get to the position I'm in now. Also having a genuine interest in the job area really helps – people can see this in your eyes when you start talking about what you do and it has a very positive effect."

"Just do it! Protecting humans, animals and the environment is too important to leave to those able to pursue the issues in full-time, paid careers."

Patrick Smith

Sheila Clifford

"A huge chunk of your life is spent working, so find something you really love doing. I have changed my career drastically – but I did it on a voluntary basis at first, so that I could get a taste of it to start with. Don't expect any job to be a bed of roses – I sometimes wonder why I did it: less money, more hours, no more sitting down all day, then I talk to a satisfied customer and I know it's all worthwhile."

Dr Alan Knight, OBE

"Go for it, control your own agenda, be outspoken, believe in your own values, but keep respect for the commercial agenda, it's your best friend!"

Chris Laughton

"When you have an inkling of what you might want to do try meeting people that already do it and even better volunteer for a while. There are few formal training courses that prepare you for the world of business and most of the skills needed are accumulated by experience, not in a classroom. At the time of writing there is a manual skills shortage and this will continue for many years. Think less about your CV and more about who to see."

"Live your life
Know that you can do it
With love all things are possible
Follow your path with heart"

David Blair

"Consider moving into the 'mainstream' and organisations that are either taking sustainability forward to some extent or those that don't realise it's an issue. Balance the trade-off of being on the 'outside' expecting change, with being on the inside promoting clear thinking and action. Be part of the solution!"

Jamie Saunders

"During my five years at college, I freelanced for various companies in order to gain work experience. This was invaluable as it taught things that you do not learn about at college – the real world and commercial viability as a designer.

"Follow your heart and dreams. Try not to let money dominate what your dreams are. I feel lucky to want to get up every day and go to work. It is good to take risks in life – always make sure that they are a considered and managed risk, though as the old cliché goes... He who dares wins!"

Britta Boyer

Dale & Wyn
Garnes

"If you're thinking of doing something like this, investigate, research, examine, do your sums, get fit, plot, plan and prepare. Having done all that if you're convinced it will work – and even if you don't think it will – if it's what you really want to do, go for it."

Steve Ward

"The hardest part I think is to get the first all-important break. I think to get this you need to be really proactive. Find out which companies or organisations offer training opportunities and really go after them. Also, it is well worth sending out speculative CVs to relevant companies, perhaps offering to work as a trainee – they may be open to the idea. Don't be proud when it comes to working for only a trainee salary, the experience you get is usually worth it.

"And remember always to follow up with a letter or call, both when you've submitted a speculative CV, or after an interview. If the potential employer is worth his or her salt, they will be impressed rather than irritated by your persistence.

"Also, if you find you can't get a job, say in renewable energy, straight away, there is no harm in gaining experience in more mainstream engineering companies whilst you bide your time to apply for the right opportunities. Any form of professional engineering experience will look attractive to potential employers. Once you've got 6 months' or 1 year's experience under your belt, you will have a real advantage over other recent graduates and things should become a bit easier."

Part Three –
The directory

Using the directory

The global movement for sustainability is broad enough to encompass many organisations, some of which do not give out careers advice or offer employment or volunteer opportunities. Instead they provide information that makes it easier for you to get a job that doesn't harm the planet. This information might include details of courses, but it is also likely to list books and magazines which will develop your knowledge of a subject.

We encourage you to use this directory as a search engine. Contact the organisations listed in the sections which interest you most and find out what they have to offer. Many will be able to give you lists of potential employers, or volunteer opportunities. Take conservation, for example. There are literally hundreds of conservation projects in Britain and around the world and it would be impossible to list them all here. To avoid repeating information you could get elsewhere, we have listed some of the books on conservation available to read. Knowing your industry inside out will give you a much better chance of getting work, so use this database as a starting point from which to gather knowledge.

The Internet

The Internet can enhance your career prospects. Use it to:

- get ideas;

- get information;

- find out what's going on;

- look for job vacancies;

- 'gen' up on an organisation you want to work for;

- look for tips on writing CVs;

- find out more about a particular career;

- find out about courses and the institutions that teach them;

- order books.

There are two ways to search for careers information on the Internet.

No. 1 – Buy a copy of *UK Directory* - the essential guide for all Internet users from a newsagent; look up the employment section; find the address of one of the websites you want to visit; go to a computer, launch your internet explorer software and type in the web address you have just found.

No. 2 – Launch your Internet explorer software and type in the name of a search engine (a website which helps you look for other websites); wait for the website to appear on your screen and type in a key word like "careers" in the search box provided; look at the list that has come up on your screen and double click on a website address that interests you.

The *UK Directory* costs £2.99 (at the time of writing) and comes out once every two months. Although it will save your phone bill, it misses some sites and has others listed under the wrong categories. However, compared to a search engine it seems more comprehensive. There are literally hundreds of careers websites listed, which compares favourably to the 119 which search engine Yahoo UK delivered.

The problem with search engines is there isn't just one, and you might have to go through a few to get to the site you really want. This sort of random searching is fun when it goes quickly but if you hit a slow patch you could regret not having a trusty piece of paper in front of you. If you want to avoid this there are some search engines that search search engines (if you see what I mean). One of these is www.dogpile.com.

The advantage of a search engine is that it is international – most give you the option of a global search. A search engine is also likely to reveal some sites you may not have noticed in the directory. Some of the best, as recommended by *Internet Monthly*, are:

www.altavista.com
www.yahoo.co.uk
www.excite.co.uk
www.hotbot.com
www.askjeeves.com

There are many more and any Internet magazine will provide a more comprehensive list.

There are several types of careers websites:
• university sites, with course details and careers advice;

• general careers sites, which cover a wide range of interests;

• specific careers sites, attached to a particular industry body or professional organisation;

• employment agencies, listing job vacancies and inviting you to sign up.

One of the best websites found on a random Yahoo search was www.careersworld.net which is linked to all British universities and offers a wide ranging database of courses and articles. In the *UK Directory* www.prospects.csu.man.ac.uk is the best site for looking up postgraduate opportunities in the UK. Doing a word search is easy. Type in sustainability and the search engine comes up with over 70 taught postgraduate courses. Type in environment and it lists several hundred.

Using the UCAS website (www.ucas.ac.uk) you can do the same thing for HND and degree courses. In some ways this is much easier than looking through their book as, like the Prospects website, you can type in keywords; although you soon discover that the chances of studying sustainability at degree level are far fewer.

Other useful sites include:
• www.oneworld.org.uk for massive database of articles on sustainable careers, regularly updated job and volunteer vacancies and links to other environmental organisations;

• www.workunlimited.co.uk for the *Guardian*'s job pages and a massive archive of material;

• www.gap.org.uk for gap year activities;

• www.get.co.uk for postgraduate opportunities;

• www.mod-app.co.uk for information about the modern apprentice scheme;

• www.dfee.gov.uk for general information about the range of educational and career related schemes available;

• www.eco.org.usa if you want to find an environmental placement in the USA;

• www.ncwe.com for information about work experience.

The Jobs Communication and campaigning

Organisations

ANIMAL AID
The Old Chapel, Bradford Road,
Tonbridge, Kent TN9 1AW.
Tel. 01732 364546 **Fax.** 01732 366533.
Website. www.animalaid.org.uk
Campaigns for animal rights.

**BRITISH UNION FOR
THE ABOLITION OF VIVISECTION**
16a Crane Grove, London N7 8NN.
Tel. 020 7700 4888 **Fax.** 020 7700 4232.
email. info@buav.org
Campaigns against animal experiments.

**BROADCAST JOURNALISM
TRAINING COUNCIL**
Website. www.bjtc.org.uk
Website only for training details.

EARTH FIRST!
Cornerstone Resource Centre,
16 Sholesbroke Avenue, Leeds LS7 3HB.
Direct action campaigning group.

ECOTRIP
PO Box 22019, Brixton, London SW2
2WF.
Tel. 020 7737 2365.
Not for profit collective promoting
eco-solutions.

**ENVIRONMENTAL INVESTIGATION
AGENCY** 2nd Floor, 69-85 Old Street,
London EC1V 9HX.
Tel. 020 7490 7040 **Fax.** 020 7490 0436.
Website. www.pair.com/eia/
email. eiauk@gn.apc.org
Has some voluntary opportunities.

FRIENDS OF THE EARTH
26-28 Underwood Street, London N1 7JQ.
Tel. 020 7490 1555 **Fax.** 020 7490 0881.
Website. www.foe.co.uk
email. info@foe.co.uk
One of UK's leading campaign groups.

FRIENDS OF THE EARTH SCOTLAND
72 Newhaven Road, Edinburgh EH6 5QG.
Tel. 0131 554 9977 **Fax.** 0131 554 8656.
Website. www.foe-scotland.org.uk
email. info@foe-scotland.org.uk
General campaigning organisation.

GENETIX SNOWBALL
6 Mount Street, Manchester M2 5NS.
Tel. 0161 834 0295.
Website. www.gn.apc.org/pmhp/gs
email. genetixsnowball@onet.co.uk
Keeping the anti-GM movement going.

GREENPEACE
Canonbury Villas,
Islington, London N1 2PN.
Tel. 020 7865 8100 **Fax.** 020 7865 8200.
Website. www.greenpeace.org.uk
One of the country's biggest campaign
groups.

INSTITUTE OF PUBLIC RELATIONS
15 Northborough Street,
London EC1V 0PR.
Tel. 020 7253 5151.
Website. www.ipr.org.uk
Provides general careers information.

**NATIONAL COUNCIL FOR THE
TRAINING OF JOURNALISTS (NCTJ)**
Latton Bush Centre, Southern Way,
Harlow, Essex CM18 7BL.

Tel. 01279 430009.
Website. www.nctj.com
General careers and training advice given.

RECLAIM THE STREETS
PO Box 9656, London N4 4JY.
Tel. 020 7281 4621.
Website. www.gn.apc.org/rts
Radical grass roots and voluntary
campain group.

SCHNEWS
c/o on-the-fiddle, PO Box 2600,
Brighton, East Sussex BN2 2DX.
Tel/Fax. 01273 685913.
email. schnews@brighton.co.uk
Weekly – the news you don't see in the
papers.

THE LAND IS OURS
Box E, 111 Magdalen Road,
Oxford OX4 1RQ.
Tel. 01865 722016.
Website. www.oneworld.org/tlio/
email. office@tlio.demon.co.uk
A land rights movement for Britain.

THE WOMEN'S ENVIRONMENTAL
NETWORK
Po Box 30626, London E1 1TZ.
Tel. 020 7481 9004 **Fax.** 020 7481 9144.
Website. www.gn.apc.org/wen
Linking women, health and the
environment.

UNDERCURRENTS
16b Cherwell Street, Oxford OX4 1BG.
Tel. 01865 203662 **Fax.** 01865 243562.
Website. www.undercurrents.org
email. underc@gn.apc.org
Now dormant – video series of demos
(news TV wouldn't show).

UNDERSTANDINGBUS
Hasenheide 54, D-10967 Berlin, Germany.
Tel. 030 695 91 20 **Fax.** 030 693 53 58.
Website. www.understandingbus.de
email. info@understandingbus.de
Provides contacts for work placements.

VEGGIES CATERING CAMPAIGN
c/o The Rainbow Centre, 180 Mansfield
Road, Nottingham NG1 3HW.
Tel. 0115 958 5666.
Website. www.veggies.org.uk
Eco-catering campaign group.

VEGAN SOCIETY
Donald Watson House,
7 Battle Road, Saint Leonards-on-Sea,
East SussexTN37 7AA.
Tel. 01424 427393 **Fax.** 01424 717064.
email. info@vegansociety.com
Campaigning organisation and publisher.

Books

GLOBAL SPIN: THE CORPORATE
ASSAULT ON ENVIRONMENTALISM
Sharon Beder, Green Books,
288pp, £10.95.
How the corporate world lashed back
against environmentalists.

MARKETING WITHOUT ADVERTISING
M Phillips and S Raspberry, £13.95.
How to sell your idea without Pepsi's
marketing budget. Available from eco
logic books.

Magazines

ADBUSTERS
1243 West 7th Avenue, Vancouver,
British Columbia, Canada V6H 1B7.
Tel. 001 604 736 9401.
Website. www.adbusters.org
Campaigns against marketing of bad
products.

Conservation, ecological resoration and woodland work

Organisations

ASSOCIATION OF NATIONAL PARKS AND COUNTRYSIDE VOLUNTARY WARDENS
c/o Carol Bowman, Lake District National Park, Murley Moss, Oxenholme Road, Kendal, Cumbria LA9 7RL.
Tel. 01539 722455.

ASSOCIATION OF COUNTRYSIDE RANGERS
ILAM House, Lower Basildon, Reading, Berkshire RG8 9NE.
Tel. 01491 874814.
Website. www.ilam.co.uk
General careers advice.

BIOREGIONAL DEVELOPMENT GROUP
The Ecology Centre, Honeywood Walk, Carshalton, Surrey SM5 3NX.
Tel. 020 8773 2322.
Helps supports local charcoal making.

BRITISH TRUST FOR CONSERVATION VOLUNTEERS
36 St Mary's Street, Wallingford, Oxford, Oxon OX10 0EU.
Tel. 01491 839 766   **Fax.** 01491 839 646.
Website. www.btcv.org.uk
email. information@btcv.org.uk
Voluntary and paid opportunities. Training too.

CONSERVATION VOLUNTEERS NORTHERN IRELAND
Dendron Lodge, Clandeboye Estate BT19 1RN.
Tel. 028 91853 778.

COUNTRYSIDE AGENCY
John Dower House, Crescent Place, Cheltenham GL50 3RA.
Tel. 01242 521381   **Fax.** 01242 584270.
Website. www.countryside.gov.uk

COUNTRYSIDE COMMISSION
John Dower House, Crescent Place, Cheltenham GL50 3RA.
Tel. 01242 531381.

COUNTRYSIDE COUNCIL FOR WALES
Plas Penrhos, Ffordd Penrhos, Bangor, Gwynedd LL57 2LQ.
Tel. 01248 370444   **Fax.** 01248 355782.
Website. www.ccw.gov.uk

COUNTRYSIDE MANAGEMENT ASSOCIATION
Point Cottage, Saltram Estate, Plympton, Plymouth PL7 3UH.
Tel. 01752 338347.
General careers and vacancies information.

EARTHWATCH INSTITUTE (EUROPE)
57 Woodstock Road, Oxford OX2 6HJ.
Tel. 01865 311600   **Fax.** 01865 311383.
Website. www.earthwatch.org
email. info@uk.earthwatch.org
Working holidays on eco projects.

ENGLISH NATURE
Northminster House, Northminster Road, Peterborough PE1 1UA.
Tel. 01733 455000.
Website. www.english-nature.org.uk
Government agency with job opportunities.

FORESTRY COMMISSION PERSONNEL
Management Branch, 231 Corstorphine
Road, Edinburgh EH12 7AT.
Tel. 0131 334 0303   **Fax.** 0131 334 4473.
email. enquiries@forestry.gov.uk
For applicants to the Forestry
Commission.

FUTURE FORESTS
Hill House, Castle Cary,
Somerset BA7 7JL.
Tel. 01963 350465.
Website. www.futureforests.com

GROUNDWORK UK
85-87 Cornwall Street,
Birmingham B3 3BY.
Tel. 0121 236 8565   **Fax.** 0121 236 7356.
Website. www.groundwork.org.uk
email. info@groundwork.org.uk
Provides list of local Groundwork trusts.

INSTITUTE OF ECOLOGY AND
ENVIRONMENTAL MANAGEMENT
36 Kingfisher Court, Hambridge Road,
Newbury, Berkshire RG14 5SJ.
Tel. 01635 37715.
General careers advice.

INTERNATIONAL CENTRE FOR
CONSERVATION EDUCATION
Greenfield House, Guiting Power,
Cheltenham GL54 5TZ.
Tel. 01451 850777   **Fax.** 01451 850705.

JON WARNES
Windsor's Cottage,
Felixstowe, Suffolk IP11 9RZ.
Tel/Fax. 01394 274419.
Website.
www.woodland.fxferry.demon.co.uk
email. jon@fxferry.demon.co.uk
Woodland crafts courses, publications
and tools.

LANTRA
Royal Welsh Showground,
Llanelwedd, Builth Wells LD2 3WY.
Tel. 01982 553131   **Fax.** 01982 553923.
Website. www.lantra.co.uk
Welsh training organisation.

NATIONAL TRUST
36 Queen Anne's Gate,
London SW1H 9AS.
Tel. 020 7222 9251.
Website. www.nationaltrust.org.uk
Trainee opportunities.

PLANTLIFE
21 Elizabeth Street, London SW1W 9RP.
Tel. 020 7808 0100   **Fax.** 020 7730 8377.
Website. www.plantlife.org.uk
email. enquiries@plantlife.org.uk
Volunteer opportunities to protect
landscape.

RAINFOREST FOUNDATION UK
Suite A5, City Cloisters,
188/196 Old Street, London EC1V 9FR.
Tel. 0207 251 6345.
Website. www.rainforestfoundationuk.org

REFORESTING SCOTLAND
21a Coates Crescent, Edinburgh EH3 7AF.
Tel. 0131 226 2496.
Website.
www.gn.apc.org/reforestingscotland
email. reforscot@gn.apc.org
Volunteer opportunities in native
woodlands.

ROYAL SOCIETY FOR NATURE
CONSERVATION AND WILDLIFE TRUSTS
The Green, Witham Park,
Waterside South, Lincoln LN5 7RJ.
Tel. 01522 544400.
Manages local wildlife reserves.

ROYAL SOCIETY FOR THE
PROTECTION OF BIRDS
The Lodge, Sandy,
Bedfordshire SG19 2DL.
Tel. 01767 680551.
Voluntary and paid opportunities.

SCOTTISH CONSERVATION
PROJECTS TRUST
Ballalan House,
24 Allan Park, Stirling FK8 2QG.
Tel. 01786 479697.
email. scp@btcv.org.uk
Voluntary and paid opportunities.

SCOTTISH WILDLIFE TRUST LTD
Cramond House, Kirk Cramond,
Cramond Glebe Road,
Edinburgh EH4 6NS.
Tel. 0131 312 7765.
Website. www.swt.org.uk
Voluntary and paid opportunities.

THE DUN BEAG PROJECT
c/o David Blair, Dun Beag,
Tighnabruaich, Argyll PA21 2DU.
Tel. 01700 811809.
Woodland conservation project.

TREES FOR LIFE
The Park, Findhorn Bay, Forres IV36 3TZ.
Tel. 01309 691292 **Fax.** 01309 691155.
Website. www.treesforlife.org.uk

WOODLAND TRUST
Autumn Park, Grantham,
Lincolnshire NG31 6LL.
Tel. 01746 581111.
Voluntary and occasional paid
opportunities.

Books

GREEN VOLUNTEERS – THE WORLD
GUIDE TO VOLUNTARY WORK IN
NATURE CONSERVATION
Green Volunteers, Vacation Work
Publications, 1999, 272pp, £10.99.
Guide to worldwide voluntary
opportunities.

WOODLANDS
BTCV, BTCV, 1988, 172pp, £9.99.
A valuable book on practical woodland
management.

Magazines

COUNTRYSIDE JOBS SERVICE
Groves Bank, Sleights,
Whitby, Noth Yorkshire YO21 1RY.
Tel. 01947 810220.
Website.
www.countrysidejobs.freeserve.co.uk
Weekly jobs listing.

ENVIRONMENT POST
See General Careers

NETWORK 21
The Conservation Foundation,
1 Kensington Gore, London SW7 2AR.
Tel. 020 7591 3111 **Fax.** 020 7591 3100.
Website.
www.conservationfoundation.co.uk
email. network21@gn.apc.org
News of conservation projects.

Construction

Organisations

ARCHITECTURAL ASSOCIATION
34-36 Bedford Square,
London WC1B 3ES.
Tel. 020 7636 0974   **Fax.** 020 7414 0782.
Website. www.architect.co.uk
email. arch-assoc@arch-assoc.org.uk
Provides good free careers literature.

ASSOCIATION FOR ENVIRONMENT CONSCIOUS BUILDERS
Nant-Y-Garreg, Seron, Llandysul,
Carmarthenshire, Wales SA44 5EJ.
TelFax. 01559 370 908.
Website. www.aecb.net
email. admin@aecb.net
Check out their directory – it contains a
list of eco-builders. Their magazine is also
useful.

BRITISH EARTH SHELTERING ASSOCIATION
100 The Crofts, Witney, Oxon OX8 7AG.
Tel. 01993 703619   **Fax.** 01993 704619.
Promotes concept of Earth sheltered
buildings.

BRITISH STRAW BALE BUILDING ASSOCIATION
5 Chataway House,
Crumpsall, Manchester M8 5UU.
Tel. 0161 202 3566.
Website.
www.users.globalnet.co.uk/~straw
email. straw@globalnet.co.uk
Information, courses, resources and
newsletter.

BUILDING AND SOCIAL HOUSING FOUNDATION
Memorial Square, Coalville,
Leicester, Leicestershire LE67 3TU.
Tel. 01530 510444   **Fax.** 01530 510332.
Website. www.bshf.org
email. bshf@compuserve.com
Researches sustainable housing.

BUILDING RESEARCH ENERGY CONSERVATION SUPPORT UNIT
Bucknalls Land, Garston,
Watford, Hertfordshire WD2 7JR.
Tel. 01923 664000   **Fax.** 01923 664097.
Website. www.bre.co.uk
email. bre@bre.co.uk
Information about energy conservation in
buildings.

COMMUNITY SELF BUILD SCOTLAND
Queenslie Business Centre,
19 Blairtummock Road, Glasgow G33 4AN.
Tel. 0141 766 1999   **Fax.** 0141 766 1888.
Website. www.cableinet.co.uk/users/csbs
email. cbs@cableinet.co.uk
Advice on community self-build projects.

CONSTRUCTION INDUSTRY ENVIRONMENTAL FORUM
6 Storey's Gate, London SW1P 3AU.
Tel. 020 7222 8891   **Fax.** 020 7222 1708.
Website. www.ciria.org.uk
email. enquiries@circia.org.uk
Offers advice on building and
construction.

CONSTRUCTIVE INDIVIDUALS
70a Holgate Road, York YO24 4AB.
Tel. 01904 625300   **Fax.** 01904 625 301.
Website. www.constructive.mcmail.com

email. constructive@mcmail.com
Community building and self-build projects.

ECOLOGICAL DESIGN ASSOCIATION
The British School, Slad Road,
Stroud, Gloucester GL5 1QW.
Tel. 01453 765 575   **Fax.** 01453 759 211.
Promotes design and use of eco-friendly materials and products. Buy their magazine.

HOCKERTON HOUSING PROJECT
2 Mystery Hill, Gables Drive, Hockerton,
Southwell, Nottinghamshire NG25 0QU.
Tel. 01636 816902.
email. nwhite@fatmac.demon.co.uk
Eco-homes tour available on request (fee).

ROYAL INSTITUTE OF BRITISH ARCHITECTS
Education Department (RIBA),
66 Portland Place, London W1N 4AD.
Tel. 020 7580 5533   **Fax.** 020 7255 1541.
Website. www.riba.org
email. @inst.riba.org
Provides information about environmentally conscious architecture.

THE CHARTERED INSTITUTE OF BUILDING SERVICES ENGINEERS
Delta House, 222 Balham High Road,
London, SW12 9BS.
Tel. 020 8675 5211   **Fax.** 020 8675 5449.
Website. www.cibse.org
email. secretary@cibse.org
Offers publications, courses and conferences.

THE COMMUNITY SELF BUILD AGENCY
40 Bowling Green Lane,
London EC1R 0NE.
Tel. 020 7415 7092   **Fax.** 020 7415 7142.
Advice on community self-build projects.

THE YOUNG BUILDERS TRUST
Massey's Folly, Church Road, Upper
Farrington, Alton, Hampshire GU34 3EG.
Tel. 01420 588 665.

WALTER SEGAL SELF BUILD TRUST
Unit 213, 16 Baldwins Gardens,
London EC1N 7RJ.
Tel. 020 7831 5696   **Fax.** 020 7831 5697.
email. wssbt@powernet.co.uk
Helps people to self-build their own homes.

WOMEN'S EDUCATION IN BUILDING
12-14 Malton Road, London W10 5UP.
Tel. 020 8968 9139   **Fax.** 020 8964 0255.
Training and volunteer placements.

Books

THE NEW NATURAL HOUSE BOOK
Pearson, Conran Octopus,
1998, 304pp, £16.99.
How to create an ecologically sound home.

THE WHOLE HOUSE BOOK:
ECOLOGICAL BUILDING DESIGN AND MATERIALS
Borer and Harris, The Centre for
Alternative Technology, 1998, 330pp,
£29.95.
All you need to know about eco-building.

Magazines

ARCHITECTS JOURNAL
151 Rosebery Avenue, London EC1R 4QX.
Tel. 020 7505 6700   **Fax.** 020 7505 6701.
Weekly general trade magazine; keeps you informed.

BUILDING FOR A FUTURE
Nant-Y-Garreg, Saron, Llandysul,
Carmarthenshire SA44 5EJ.
Tel. 01559 370908   **Fax.** 01559 370908.
Website.
http://members.aol.com/buildgreen
email. buildgreen@aol.com
Keeps you in touch with latest developments.

ECO DESIGN
The British School, Slad Road,
Stroud, Gloucstershire GL5 1QW.
Tel. 01453 765575   **Fax.** 01453 759211.
The design magazine to get – always inspiring.

ENERGY IN BUILDINGS AND INDUSTRY
8th Floor, Tubs Hill House, London Road,
Sevenoaks, Kent TN13 1BL.
Tel. 01732 464154   **Fax.** 01732 464454.
email. eibi.insidecome.co.uk
Monthly energy use magazine for professionals.

SELF BUILD
The Well House, High Street,
Burton-on-Trent, Staffordshire DE14 1JQ.
Tel. 01283 742950   **Fax.** 01283 742966.
Useful if you want to build your own
home.

SUSTAIN
McClennand Publishing, Rational House,
64 Bridge Street, Manchester M3 3BN.
Tel. 0161 950 4500   **Fax.** 0161 950 4514.
email. sustain@mcpub.u-net.com
Sustainable building magazine – industry
bias.

SUSTAINABLE BUILDING – AN
INDEPENDENT JOURNAL ON BUILDING
AND THE ENVIRONMENT.
AENEAS technical publishers,
PO Box 356, 5680 AJ Best,
The Netherlands.
Tel. +499 335833   **Fax.** +499 335830.
An industry-orientated magazine with
news and features.

THE LAST STRAW
HC66 Box 119, Hillsboro, NM 88042,
USA.
Website. www.strawhomes.com
email. the laststraw@strawhomes.com
America's leading straw bale magazine.

Creative art and design

Organisations

ARTS COUNCIL OF GREAT BRITAIN
14 Great Peter Street, London SW1P 3NQ.
Tel. 020 7333 0100.
Website. www.artscouncil.org.uk

ARTS COUNCIL OF NORTHERN IRELAND
MacNeice House, 77 Malone Road,
Belfast BT9 6AQ.
Tel. 028 90385200.

ARTS COUNCIL OF WALES
9 Museum Place, Cardiff CF1 3LN.
Tel. 029 20376500.

BRITISH INSTITUTE OF PROFESSIONAL PHOTOGRAPHY
Fox Talbot House, Amwell End,
Ware, Hertfordshire SG12 9HN.
Tel. 01920 464011.
Website. www.eipp.com
Details of training.

BRITTA BOYER
Tel. 07930 581004.
Fashion designer working with eco materials.

CAPITB TRUST
80 Richardshaw Lane,
Pudsey, Leeds LS28 6BN.
Tel. 0113 239 3355.
Website. www.careers-in-clothing.co.uk
General careers information.

CENTRE FOR SUSTAINABLE DESIGN
Falkner Road, Farnham, Surrey GU9 7DS.
Tel. 01252 892 773.
Website. www.cfsd.org.uk

CRAFTS COUNCIL
44a Pentonville Road, London N1 9HF.
Tel. 020 7806 2500.
Website. www.craftscouncil.org.uk

DESIGN COUNCIL
34 Bow Street,
Covent Garden, London WC2E 7DL.
Tel. 020 7420 5200.
Website. www.design-council.org.uk
General careers information.

ECO DESIGN
See Architecture and Building

ECOLOGICAL DESIGN INITIATIVE
245 Gate Five Road,
Sausalito, CA 94965, USA.
Website. www.ecodesign.org

ENVIRO ARTS
Website.
www.envirolink.org/enviroarts/content
Website for environmental artists

GREEN FIBRES
Freepost Lon 7805(C),
Totnes, Devon TQ9 5ZZ.
Tel. 1803868001 **Fax.** 1803868002.
Website. www.greenfibres.com
email. greenfibre@aol.com
Get some inspiration from their catalogue.

HEMP UNION
24 Anlaby Road, Hull HU1 2PA.
Tel. 01482 225328.
Website. www.karoo.netlhemp-union
Interesting selection of hemp products.

NATURAL COLLECTION
Box 2111, Bath BA1 2ZQ.

Tel. 01225 442288   **Fax.** 01225 469673.
Website. www.ecostore.co.uk/eco.html
Get some inspiration from their catalogue.

PLATFORM
7 Horselydown Lane, London SE1 2LN.
Tel. 020 7403 3738.
Theme based arts projects.

RURAL CRAFTS ASSOCIATION
Brook Road, Wormley,
Godalming, Surrey GU8 5UA.
Tel. 01428 682292   **Fax.** 01428 685969.
email.
RuralCraftsAssociation@btinternet.com
Produces a 2000 year planner.

SCOTTISH ARTS COUNCIL
12 Manor Place, Edinburgh EH3 7DD.
Tel. 0131 226 6051.
Website. www.sac.org.uk

SCOTTISH ECOLOGICAL
DESIGN ASSOCIATION
11 Inveresk Village, Musselburgh,
East Lothian EH21 7TD.
Tel. 0131 665 8867.

SOCIETY FOR RESPONSIBLE DESIGN
PO Box 288, Marion Street, Leichardt,
New South Wales, 2040 Australia.
Tel. 00 61 29564 0721.

TEXTILE ENVIRONMENT NETWORK
c/o National Centre for Business and
Ecology, Peel Building, University of
Salford, Manchester M5 4WT.
Tel. 0161 295 5276.
email. mailbase@mailbase.ac.uk

THE CRAFTS MOVEMENT
PO Box 1641 Frome, Somerset BA11 1YY.
Tel. 01373 813333.
Holds fairs across Britain.

VIRTUAL CRAFT FAIR
Website. www.craftville.com
Show your crafts on the web.

Books

DESIGN COURSES IN BRITAIN
Various authors, Trotman and Co,
Annual, Page length varies, £11.50.
Full listing.

GREEN DESIGN
Mackenzie, Laurence King,
1997, 176pp, £19.95.
Defines the issues faced by designers.

Magazines

CRAFTS
The Craft Council,
44a Pentonville Road, London N1 9BY.
Tel. 020 7806 2542.
Website. www.craftscouncil.org.uk
Full of contacts and useful information.

ECO-DESIGN
Ecological Design Association
(see Architecture and Building).
Essential buy for eco-designers.

Development

Organisations

BRITISH COUNCIL
Bridgewater House,
58 Whitworth Street, Manchester M1 6BB.
Tel. 0161 957 7000 **Fax.** 0161 957 7111.
Website. www.britcoun.org/
email. education.enquiries@britcom.co.uk
Produces a guide to development.

BRITISH VOLUNTEER
AGENCY LIAISON GROUP OK
United Nations Association International
Service, Suite 3a, Hunter House,
57 Goodramgate, York YO1 7FX.
Tel. 01904 647 799 **Fax.** 01904 652 353.
Website. www.oneworld.org/is
email. unais-uk@geo2.poptel.org.uk
Has information about volunteer
organisations abroad.

DEPARTMENT OF
INTERNATIONAL DEVELOPMENT
94 Victoria Street, London SW1E 5JL.
Tel. 020 7917 7000 **Fax.** 020 7917 0016.
Website. www.dfid.gov.uk
Produces information about working
abroad.

GLOBAL PARTNERSHIP ASSOCIATION
PO Box 1001, London SE24 9NL.
Tel. 020 7924 0974 **Fax.** 020 7738 7512.
Holds the global partnership world fair.

INSTITUTE OF DEVELOPMENT STUDIES
University of Sussex,
Brighton, East Sussex BN1 9RE.
Tel. 01273 606261 **Fax.** 01273 691647.
Website. www.ids.ac.uk/ids
email. ids@ids.ac.uk

Research and training. Huge resource
library too.

INTERMEDIATE TECHNOLOGY
DEVELOPMENT GROUP
The Schumacher Centre for
Technology and Development,
Bourton Hall, Warwickshire CV23 9QZ.
Tel. 01788 661100 **Fax.** 01788 661101.
Website. www.oneworld.org/itdg
email. enquiries@itdg.org.uk
International development agency.

INTERMEDIATE TECHNOLOGY
PUBLICATIONS
Southampton Row, London WC1B 4HH.
Tel. 020 7436 9761 **Fax.** 020 7436 2013.
Website.
www.oneworld.org/itdg/publications
email. orders@itpubs.org.uk
Biggest bookshop/mail order service in
UK.

OXFAM GB
Oxfam House,
274 Banbury Road, Oxford OX2 7DZ.
Tel. 01865 313600.
email. oxfam@oxfam.org.uk
One of Britain's largest development
charities.

POWERFUL INFORMATION
21 Church Lane,
Laughton, Milton Keynes MK5 8AS.
Tel/Fax. 01908 666 275.
Website.
www.ecosaurus.co.uk/powerful-
information
email. powerinfo@gn.apc.org
Provides training, advice and books.

RETURNED VOLUNTEER ACTION OK
1 Amwell Street, London SE5 9NR.
Tel. 020 7733 3577   **Fax.** 020 7978 8006.
Website. www.bookaid.org.uk
Takes second hand books and passes
them on to the developing world.

TECHNOLOGY EXCHANGE
Rest Park, Siloe, Bedford ML45 4HJ.
Tel. 01525 860 333.
Website. www.uktech.net

TOOLS FOR SELF RELIANCE
Netley Marsh Workshops, Netley Marsh,
Southampton, Hampshire SO40 7GY.
Tel. 023 80869 697   **Fax.** 023 80868 544.
email. tools@gn.apc.org.uk
Volunteers needed to collect and mend
tools.

WOMANKIND WORLDWIDE OK
3 Albion Place, Gelena Road,
Hammersmith, London W6 0LT.
Tel. 020 8563 8608   **Fax.** 020 8563 8611.
Website. www.oneworld.org/womankind

WORLD SOLAR PROGRAMME
UNESCO, 7 Place de Fontenoy,
75352 Paris 07 SP, France.
Tel. 00 33 1 45 68 10 00.
Fax. 00 33 1 45 67 16 90.
Website. www.unesco.org/science/wssp
Promotes adoption of renewable energy
sources.

Books

SHARING THE WORLD:
SUSTAINABLE LIVING AND
GLOBAL EQUITY IN THE 21ST CENTURY
Carley and Spapens,
Earthscan, 208pp, £14.95.
Useful introduction to the subject.

THE BAREFOOT REVOLUTION
Bertrand Schneider, Intermediate
Technology, 1988, 245pp, £12.95.
A classic text.

Magazines

APPROPRIATE TECHNOLOGY
103 -105 Southampton Row,
London WC1B 4HH.
Development magazine with job section.

Energy

Organisations

**BRITISH ASSOCIATION
OF BIOFUELS AND OILS**
Curlew Court, Guy's Head Road,
Sutton Bridge, Lincolnshire PE12 9QQ.
Tel. 01406 350848 **Fax.** 01406 351791.
email. babfo@pcleary.freeserve.co.uk
Promotes biofuels as alternative to
petroleum.

BRITISH HYDROPOWER ASSOCIATION
c/o Wilson Energy Associates,
52 Bramhall Lane South,
Bramhall, Stockport, Cheshire SK7 1AH.
Tel. 0161 440 9196 **Fax.** 0161 440 9273.
email. weal@mcmail.com
Promotes use of water power.

BRITISH PHOTOVOLTAIC ASSOCIATION
The Warren, Bramshill Road,
Eversley, Hampshire RG27 OPR.
Tel. 0118 932 4418 **Fax.** 0118 973 7315.
Website. www.pv-uk.org.uk/
email. pv-uk@dial.pipex.com
Represents the UK pv industry.

BRITISH WIND ENERGY ASSOCIATION
26 Spring Street,
Paddington, London W2 1JA.
Tel. 020 7402 7102 **Fax.** 020 7402 7107.
Website. www.bwea.com
email. bwea@gn.apc.org
Professional and trade association.

CADDET
ETSU, B 168, Harwell,
Didcot, Oxon OX11 0RA.
Tel. 01235 432719 **Fax.** 01235 433595.
Website. www.caddet-re.org

email. caddet.renew@aeat.co.uk
Free database on website.

**CENTRE FOR RENEWABLE AND
SUSTAINABLE TECHNOLOGY (CREST)**
1624 Franklin Street,
1000 Oakland, California 94612, USA.
Tel. 001 510 588 5600.
Website. www.solstice.crest.org

**COMBINED HEAT
AND POWER ASSOCIATION**
Grosvenor Gardens House, 35-37
Grosvenor Gardens, London SW1W 0BS.
Tel. 020 7828 4077 **Fax.** 020 7828 0310.
Website. www.chpa.co.uk
email. info@chpa.co.uk
Promotes district heating and CHP.

CROISSANT NEUF
Ham Mills Road, Bowlish,
Shepton Mallet, Somerset BA4 5JH.
Tel/Fax. 01749 343953.
Travelling educational circus.

ECOTRICITY
Axiom House, Station Road,
Stroud, Gloucestershire GL5 3AP.
Tel. 01453 756 111.

**ENERGY AND ENVIRONMENT
RESEARCH UNIT**
Faculty of Technology, Open University,
Walton Hall, Buckinghamshire MK7 6AA.
Tel. 01908 653335 **Fax.** 01908 653744.
Website. www-tec.open.ac.uk/eeru
email. eeru-www@open.ac.uk
R&D and education in energy use.

INSTITUTE FOR APPLIED ECOLOGY
Postfach 6226, 79038 Freiburg, Germany.

Tel. 0049 761 452950.
Website. www.oeko.de
Pioneering research into solar power.

INSTITUTE OF ENERGY
18 Devonshire Street, London W1N 2AU.
Tel. 020 7580 7124   **Fax.** 020 7580 4420.
Website. www.instenergy.org.uk
Facilitates education and training – runs
courses.

IRISH ENERGY CENTRE
Sinagh House, Bandon,
County Cork, Republic of Ireland.
Tel. +353 23 42193   **Fax.** +353 23 41304.
Website. www.irish-energy.ie/reio
Renewable energy information centre.

IRISH WIND ENERGY ASSOCIATION
Kellystown, Slane, Co. Meath, Ireland.
Tel/Fax. 00 353 41 26787.
Website. www.iwea.com
email. staudy@iol.ie
Promotes wind power in Ireland.

MIDLANDS RENEWABLE ENERGY
TECHNOLOGY TRANSFER
Whittle Hill Farm Buildings,
B5330 Road, Nanpanton,
Loughborough, Leicestershire LE12 9YE.
Tel. 01509 610033   **Fax.** 01509 610055.
Website. www.mrett.co.uk
email. jane@mrett.co.uk
Information sharing group.

NETWORK FOR ALTERNATIVE
TECHNOLOGY AND TECHNOLOGY
ASSESSMENT
c/o EERU (see above),
Promotes development of renewable
energy.

NEW AND RENEWABLE
ENERGY ENQUIRIES BUREAU
ETSU, B168, Didcot,
Harwell, Oxon OX11 ORA.
Tel. 01235 432450   **Fax.** 01235 433066.
Website. www.etsu.co.uk
email. etsu.business@aeat.co.uk
DTI funded co-ordinator of RE projects in
UK.

RENEW NORTH
Old Queen's Head Yard, 7B Oldgate,
Morpeth, Northumberland NE61 1PY.
Tel. 01670 504464   **Fax.** 01670 510300.
email. information@renewnorth.co.uk
Information sharing group.

RENEWABLE ENERGY IN THE URBAN
ENVIRONMENT
95 East Hill, Wandsworth,
London SW18 2QD.
Tel/Fax. 020 8871 4647.
email. cleanpower@renue.freeserve.co.uk
Funds renewable energy projects in
London.

ROCKY MOUNTAIN INSTITUTE
1739 Snowmass Creek Road,
Snowmass, Colorado, 81 654 9199, USA,
Tel. 001 970 927 3851.
Website. www.rmi.org
Pioneering eco power research.

SHINE 21
(SOLAR HEATING INSTALLER NETWORK)
c/o Filsol, Unit 15,
Ponthenri Industrial Estate,
Llanelli, Carmarthenshire SA15 5RA.
Tel. 01269 860229   **Fax.** 01269 860979.
Trains plumbers to install solar water
heating.

SOLAR CENTURY
Unit 5 Sandycombe Centre,
1-9 Sandycombe Road,
Kew, Richmond, Surrey TW9 2EP.
Tel. 020 8332 6565   **Fax.** 0870 735 8101.
Website. www.solarcentury.co.uk
email. webmaster@solarcentury.co.uk
Heads a solar task force in Britain.

SOLAR TRADE ASSOCIATION
Pengillan, Lerryn,
Lostwithiel, Cornwall PL22 0QE.
Tel/Fax. 01208 873 518.
Maintains standards and promotes solar.

SOUTH MIDLANDS
RENEWABLE ENERGY ADVICE CENTRE
3 Benbow Court, Shenley Church End,
Milton Keynes, Bucks. MK5 6JG.
Tel. 01908 501 908   **Fax.** 01908 504 848.
Website. www.natenergy.org.uk/smreac
email. smreac@natenerg.demon.co.uk
Information sharing group.

SOUTHAMPTON UNIVERSITY,
SOLAR ENERGY CENTRE
Department of Engineering,
University of Southampton,
Southampton, Hampshire S017 1BJ.
Tel. 023 80593783   **Fax.** 023 80593016.
Website. www.sotan.ac.uk/~solar
email. t.markvart@soton.ac.uk

Organises summer school on solar
electiricty.

THE WIND FUND
Brunel House, 11 The Promenade,
Clifton, Bristol BS8 3NN.
Tel. 0800 056 2761.
Website. www.windfund.co.uk
Offers funds for wind energy projects.

UK-ISES
(INTERNATIONAL SOLAR ENERGY
SOCIETY)
School of Engineering, Oxford Brookes
University, Gipsy Lane Campus,
Headington, Oxford OX3 0BP.
Tel. 01865 484367   **Fax.** 01865 484263.
Website. www.brookes.ac.uk/uk-ises
email. uk-ises@brookes.ac.uk
Promotes solar power in Britain.

THE SOLAR DESIGN COMPANY
c/o Chris Laughton, 57 Wood Lane,
Greasby, Wirral CH49 2PU.
Tel. 0151 606 0207
Case study Chris Laughton.

Books

RENEWABLE ENERGY:
POWER FOR A SUSTAINABLE FUTURE
Ed. Godfrey Boyle, Open University Press,
1996, 479pp, £24.95.
The guide for undergraduates.

SOLAR LIVING SOURCE BOOK
Schaeffer and Real Goods Staff,
Real Goods, 1996, 700pp, £25.00.
Complete guide to renewable
technologies.

Magazines

BIOMASS FARMER AND USER
The Green, Calne, Wiltshire SN11 8DL.
Tel. 01249 821242   **Fax.** 01249 814155.
email. gmacpherson@cix.compulink.co.uk
For producers and processors of energy
crops.

BIOMASS FOCUS
New and Renewable Energy
Enquiries Bureau, ETSU, Harwell,
Oxfordshire OX11 ORA.
Tel. 012345 432450.
Industry magazine published by the DTI.

CADDET RENEWABLE
ENERGY NEWSLETTER
Centre for Renewable Energy,
ETSU, Harwell, Oxfordshire OX11 ORA.
Tel. 01235 432158   **Fax.** 01235 432331.
Website. www.caddet-re.org
email. nick.hall-stride@aeat.co.uk
Covers energy and environmental issues.

FUEL CELLS UK NEWSLETTER
ETSU, Harwell, Didcot, Oxon OX11 0RA.
Tel. 01235 432450   **Fax.** 01235 433066.
Government magazine on fuel cells.

NEW ENERGY (NEUE ENERGIE)
Bundesverband WindEnergie, Redaktaion
'New Energy', Herrenteichsstr. 1,
D-49074 Osnabruck, Deustchland.
Tel/Fax. +49 0 541 35060 30.
email. NE-BWE@t-online.de
Gives you the international perspective.

NEW REVIEW
ETSU, Harwell, Didcot, Oxon OX11 0RA.
Tel. 01235 432450   **Fax.** 01235 433066.
Website. www.dti.gov.uk/NewReview
Newsletter for renewables industry.

RENEW
Faculty of Technology,
The Open University,
Walton Hall, Milton Keynes,
Buckinghamshire MK7 6AA.
Tel. 01908 654368   **Fax.** 01908 653744.
Website.
www.tec.open.ac.uk/eeru/natta/rol
email. S.J.Dougan@open.ac.uk
News and features about renewable
energy.

RENEW
PO Box 2001, Lygon Street North,
Brunswick East, VIC 3057, Australia.
Website. www.ata.org.au
email. ata@ata.org.au
Renewables view from down under.

RENEWABLE ENERGY REPORT
Financial Times Business Ltd,
Maple House, 149 Tottenham Court Road,
London W1P 9LL.
Tel. 020 7896 2275.
Coverage of global renewables industry.

RENEWABLE ENERGY WORLD
5th Floor, 35-37 Williams Road,
London NW1 3ER.
Tel. 020 7387 8558   **Fax.** 020 7387 8998.

Website. www.jxj.com
email. rew@jxj.com
Covers industry developments.

SOLAR ENERGY
Elsevier House, The Boulevard, Langford
Lane, Kidlington, Oxford OX5 1GB.
Tel. 01865 843000 **Fax.** 01865 843010.
Website.
www.elsevier.nl/wordlocate/solener
For scientists, engineers and
technologists.

SUSTAINABLE ENERGY DEVELOPMENT
GSR Publications, 72C Old Dover Road,
Blackheath, London SE3 8SY.
Tel. 020 8305 1831.
Industry magazine with news and
features.

THE SUSTAINABLE
ENERGY INDUSTRY JOURNAL
European Media Marketing Ltd,
Publications Department,
PO Box 259, Bromley BR1 1ZR.
Tel. 020 8289 8989 **Fax.** 020 8289 8484.
Website. www.emml.com
email. journal@emml.co.uk
The title says it all.

WIND DIRECTIONS
26 Spring Street, London W2 1JA.
Tel. 020 7202 7122 **Fax.** 020 7402 7125.
email. ewea@compuserve.com
Covers developments in the wind industry.

WIND POWER MONTHLY
PO Box 100, DK-8420 Knebel, Denmark.
Tel. +45 86 365 900
Fax. +45 86 365 626.
Website. www.windpower-monthly.com
email. mail@windpower-monthly.com
International news on wind power.

Energy conservation, waste minimisation and recycling

Organisations

ASSOCIATION FOR THE CONSERVATION OF ENERGY
Westgate House,
Preband Street, London N1 8PT.
Tel. 020 7359 8000 **Fax.** 020 7359 0863.
Website.
members.aol.com/aceuk/home.html
email. aceuk@aol.com
Organises training in energy conservation.

CENTRE FOR RESEARCH EDUCATION AND TRAINING IN ENERGY
Kenley House, 25 Bridgeman Terrace,
Wigan, Lancashire WN1 1TD.
Tel. 01942 322271 **Fax.** 01942 322273.
Website. www.create.org.uk
email. info@create.org.uk
Compiles a directory of energy trainers.

CENTRE FOR SUSTAINABLE ENERGY
CREATE Centre, B-Bond Warehouse,
Smeaton Road, Bristol BS1 6XN.
Tel. 0117 929 9950 **Fax.** 0117 929 9114.
Website. www.cse.org.uk
email. cse@cse.org.uk
Training in energy conservation.

COMMUNITY COMPOSTING NETWORK
67 Alexandra Road, Sheffield S2 3EE.
Tel. 0114 258 0483.

COMMUNITY RECYCLING NETWORK
10-12 Picton Street,
Montpelier, Bristol BS6 5QA.
Tel. 0117 942 0142.
Website. www.crnhq.demon.co.uk

ENERGY SYSTEMS TRADE ASSOCIATION
PO Box 77, Benfleet, Essex SS7 5EX.

Tel. 07041 492049 **Fax.** 01453 492050.
Website. www.esta.org.uk
email. info@esta.org.uk
Produces directory of members.

ENVIRON
Parkfield, Weston House,
Hinckley Road, Leicester LE3 6HX.
Tel. 0016 222 0222.
Website. www.sustainability.org/

ENVIRONMENT TECHNOLOGY BEST PRACTICE PROGRAMME
Tel. 0800 585794.
Website. www.etsu.com/etbpp

ENVIRONMENT, ENERGY AND WASTE DIRECTORATE
DETR, Ashdown House, SW1E 3DE.
Tel. 020 7890 3000 **Fax.** 020 7890 6659.
Website.
www.environment.detr.gov.uk/greening
Government body with many responsibilities.

EXTERNAL WALL INSULATION ASSOCIATION
PO Box 12, Halesmere, Surrey GU27 3AH.
Tel. 01428 654011 **Fax.** 01428 651401.
Website. www.nationline.co.uk
email. theceed@compuserve.com
Creates technical, ethical and legal standards.

NATIONAL ENERGY FOUNDATION
The National Energy Centre, Davy Avenue,
Knowlhill, Milton Keynes MK5 8NG.
Tel. 0800 512012 or 01908 665555.
Fax. 01908 665577.
Website. www.natenergy.org.uk

email. nef@natenerg.demon.co.uk
Lots of information about energy
conservation.

THE ENERGY SAVINGS TRUST
21 Dartmouth Street, London SW1H 9BP.
Tel. 020 7222 0101   **Fax.** 020 7654 2444.
Website. www.est.org.uk
Manages energy efficiency schemes in
UK.

WASTE MANAGEMENT
INFORMATION BUREAU
AEA Technology,
National Environmental Centre,
Abingdon, Culham, Oxon OX14 3ED.
Tel. 01235 463162   **Fax.** 01235 463004.
Website. www.aeat-env.com
email. wmib@aeat.co.uk
Provides information on waste
management.

WASTE WATCH
Europa House, 13-17 Ironmonger Road,
London, EC1V 3QG.
Tel. 020 7253 6266   **Fax.** 020 7248 1404.
Website. www.wastewatch.org.uk
Supports community recycling projects.

Tonbridge, Kent TN9 1DH.
Tel. 01732 368333   **Fax.** 01732 368337.
Website. www.wrf.org.uk
email. wrf@wrf.org.uk
News on recycling and waste
management.

WASTE WATCH REVIEW
Europa House, Ground Floor,
13-17 Ironmonger Row,
London EC1V 3QG.
Round up of waste management news.

Books

ECO-RENOVATION
Edward Harland, Green Books,
1993, 256pp, £9.95.
Practical energy conservation book for
home owners.

FACTOR FOUR
Weizsacker, Lovins and Lovins,
Earthscan, 1997, 322pp, £12.00.
Thorough explanation of why efficiency
counts.

Magazines

SUSTAINABLE ENERGY DEVELOPMENTS
GSR Publications, 72C Old Dover Road,
Blackheath, London SE3 8SY.
Tel. 020 8305 1831   **Fax.** 020 8305 1831.
email. gail.rajgor@lineone.net
Promotes energy efficiency.

WARMER BULLETIN – JOURNAL FOR
SUSTAINABLE WASTE MANAGEMENT
Heath House, 133 High Street,

Engineering

Organisations

ENGINEERING AND MARINE TRAINING AUTHORITY
Emta house, 14 Upton Road,
Watford, Hertfordshire WD1 7EP.
Tel. 01923 238 441   **Fax.** 01923 256 086.
Website. www.emta.org.uk
email. customercare@emta.org.uk
National Training Organisation.

ENGINEERING COUNCIL
10 Maltravers Street, London WC2R 3ER.
Tel. 020 7240 7891   **Fax.** 020 7240 7517.
Website. www.engc.org.uk
email. webmaster@engc.org.uk
Helps students get into engineering.

INSTITUTE OF CHEMICAL ENGINEERS
Davis Building, 165-189 Railway Terrace,
Rugby, Warwickshire CV21 3HQ.
Tel. 01788 578214   **Fax.** 01788 560833.
Website. www.icheme.org
email. she@icheme.org.uk
General careers information and course list.

INSTITUTE OF CIVIL ENGINEERS
1 Great George Street,
London SW1P 3AA.
Tel. 020 7222 7722   **Fax.** 020 7222 7500.
Website. www.ice.org.uk
General advice on careers and courses.

INSTITUTE OF ELECTRICAL ENGINEERS
Savoy Place, London WC2R OBL.
Tel. 020 7240 1871   **Fax.** 020 7497 3609.
Website. www.iee.org.uk
email. scholarships@iee.org.uk
Provides educational and careers material.

INSTITUTE OF MATERIALS
1 Carlton House Terrace,
London SW1Y 5DB.
Tel. 020 7839 4071   **Fax.** 020 7839 1702
Website. www.materials.org.uk
email. admin@materials.org.uk
Lists of college courses, videos and publications.

INSTITUTE OF MECHANICAL ENGINEERS
Northgate Avenue,
Bury St Edmonds, Suffolk IP32 6BN.
Tel. 01284 763277   **Fax.** 01284 704006.
Website. www.imeche.org.uk
email. enquiries@imeche.org.uk
Publications on courses and careers.

INSTITUTION OF INCORPORATED ENGINEERS
Savoy Hill House,
Savoy Hill, London WC2R OBS.
Tel. 020 7836 3357   **Fax.** 020 7497 9006.
Website. www.iie.org.uk
email. iee@dial.pipex.com
Prints a number of useful careers leaflets.

Local and national government

Organisations

CAPITA RAS
Innovation Court, New Street,
Basingstoke, Hampshire RG2 7JB.
Tel. 01275 383683 **Fax.** 01256 383780.
Website.
www.rasnet.co.uk/RAS/capitaras.html
Handles recruitment into civil service.

**GRADUATE AND SCHOOLS
LIAISON BRANCH**
Cabinet Office, Office of Public Service,
Horse Guards Road, London SW1P 3AL.
Tel. 020 7270 5034.
Information about working in civil service.

**LOCAL GOVERNMENT NATIONAL
TRAINING ORGANISATION**
Layden House,
76-86 Turnhill Street, London EC1M 5LG.
Tel. 0207 296 6600.
Information about training.

ROYAL TOWN PLANNING INSTITUTE
26 Portland Place, London W1N 4BE.
Tel. 020 7636 9107 **Fax.** 020 7323 1583.
Website. www.rtpi.org.uk
Advice about careers and courses.

**THE LOCAL GOVERNMENT
MANAGEMENT BOARD**
Local Government Opportunities,
Layden House, 76-86 Turnmill Street,
London EC1M 5QU.
Tel. 020 7296 6503.
Website. www.lgmb.gov.uk
General careers advice.

Magazines

PUBLIC SECTOR
ORP Direct Ltd, PO Box 152,
Tunbridge Wells, Kent TN4 9ZW.
Tel. 01892 511667.
Magazine for those working in the public
sector.

TOWN AND COUNTRY PLANNING
17 Carlton House Terrace,
London SW1Y 5AS.
Tel. 020 7930 8903 **Fax.** 020 7930 3280.
Website. www.tcpa.org.uk
email. editor@tcpa.org.uk
Sets out the planning agenda – very good.

Organic growing

Organisations

AGRICULTURAL TRAINING BOARD (ATB LANDBASE)
National Agriculture Centre,
Kenilworth, Warwickshire CV8 2LG.
Tel. 024 76 696996/0345 078007
Fax. 024 76 696732.
Website. www.lantra.co.uk
Training organisation – some organic
information.

BIO-DYNAMIC AGRICULTURAL ASSOCIATION
Painswick Inn Project,
Stroud, Glos. GL5 1QG.
Tel/Fax. 01453 759501.
Website. www.anth.org.uk/biodynamic
email. bdaa@biodynamic.freeserve.co.uk
Teaches alternative planting methods.

OTLEY COLLEGE
Otley, Ipswich, Suffolk IP6 9EY.
Tel. 01473 785543   **Fax.** 01473 785353.
Website. www.otleycollege.ac.uk
General careers advice about
landscaping.

CAMPHILL VILLAGE TRUST
Delrow House, Hilfield Lane, Aldenham,
Watford, Hertfordshire WD2 8DJ.
Tel. 01923 856006   **Fax.** 01923 858035.
email. email@dalrow.newnet.co.uk
Volunteers needed to work with
handicapped.

COMMON GROUND
PO Box 25309, London NW5 12A.
Tel. 020 7627 2144.
Website. www.commonground.org.uk
Community land projects.

ELM FARM RESEARCH CENTRE
Hamstead Marshall,
Newbury, Berkshire RG20 0HR.
Tel. 01488 658 298   **Fax.** 01488 658 503.
email. 100113.751@compuserve.com
Offers advice and research findings to
farmers.

FARMERS LINK
49A High Street,
Watton, Thetford, Norfolk IP25 6AP.
Tel. 01953 889100.

FEDERATION OF CITY FARMS AND COMMUNITY GARDENS
The Greenhouse, Hereford Street,
Bedminster, Bristol BS3 4NA.
Tel. 0117 923 1800   **Fax.** 0117 923 1900.
email. FarmGarden@internet.com

FOOD POVERTY NETWORK
94 White Lion Street, London N1 9PF.
Tel. 0207 837 1228.
Website.
www.users.charity.vfree.com/s/sustain

HENRY DOUBLEDAY RESEARCH ASSOCIATION
Ryton Organic Gardens,
Coventry CV8 3LG.
Tel. 024 7630 3517   **Fax.** 024 7630 9229.
Website. www.hdra.org.uk
email. enquiry@hdra.org.uk
The organic gardeners association of
Britain.

THRIVE
(FORMERLY HORTICULTURAL THERAPY)
The Geoffrey Udall Centre,
Beach Hill, Reading, Somerset RG7 2AT.

Tel. 0118 9885688   **Fax.** 0118 9885677.
Website. www.thrive.org.uk
email. info@thrive.org.uk
Gardening for people with special needs.

INSTITUTE OF HORTICULTURE
14-15 Belgrave Square,
London SW1X 8PS.
Tel/Fax. 020 7245 6943.
Website. www.horticulture.demon.co.uk
email. ioh@horticulture.org.uk
General careers information.

NATIONAL SOCIETY OF
ALLOTMENT AND LEISURE GARDENERS
Odell House, Hunters Road,
Corby, Northants. NN17 5JE.
Tel. 01536 266576   **Fax.** 01536 264509.
Find out about allotment gardening.

ORGANIC CONVERSION
INFORMATION CENTRE
Soil Association, Bristol House,
40-56 Victoria Street, Bristol BS1 6BY.
Tel. 0117 929 0661   **Fax.** 0117 925 2504.
Website. www.soilassociation.org
email. info@soilassociation.org
Provides training and marketing help.

ORGANIC FOOD
AND FARMING CENTRE
Soil Association, Bristol House,
40-56 Victoria Street BS1 6BY.
Tel. 0117 929 0661   **Fax.** 0117 925 2504.
Website. www.soilassociation.org
email. info@soilassociation.org
Information centre for consumers and
producers.

ORGANICS DIRECT
7 Willow Street, London EC2A 4BH.
Tel. 020 7729 2828.
Website. www.organicsdirect.com
Organic food delivered by post.

PERMACULTURE ASSOCIATION
BCM Permaculture Association,
London WC1N 3XX.
Tel/Fax. 07041 390170.
Website. www.permaculture.org.uk
email. office@permaculture.org.uk
Supports Britain's permaculture
movement.

PLANTS FOR A FUTURE
The Field, Higher Penpol,
Lostwithiel, Cornwall PL22 ONG.
Tel. 01208 972963.

Website. www.scs.leeds.ac.uk/pfaf
email. pfaf@scs.leeds.ac.uk
Pioneers the use of perennial edible
plants.

REAL FOODS
37 Broughton Street, Edinburgh EH1 3JU.
Tel. 0131 557 1911   **Fax.** 0131 558 3530.
Website. www.realfoods.co.uk

ROYAL BOTANICAL GARDENS
Kew, Richmond, Surrey TW9 3AB.
Tel. 0208 332 5622.
Website. www.rbgkew.org.uk
Respected training, but not specifically
organic.

ROYAL HORTICULTURAL
SOCIETY GARDEN
Wisley, Woking, Surrey GU23 6QB.
Tel. 01483 224234.
Respected training, but not specifically
organic.

RURAL AGRICULTURAL AND ALLIED
WORKERS, TRANSPORT AND GENERAL
WORKERS UNION
Transport House, 128 Theobold's Road,
Holborn, London WC1 8TN.
Tel. 020 76112500   **Fax.** 020 76112555.
email. tgwu@tgwu.org.uk
General careers advice.

SCOTTISH FEDERATION
OF COMMUNITY FOOD INITIATIVES
c/o Money Matters,
986-988 Govan Road, Glasgow G51.
Tel. 0141 445 5221.

SUNSEED TANZANIA TRUST
8 Marchmont Crescent,
Edinburgh EH9 1HN.
Tel/Fax. 0131 229 4586.
Website. www.sunseed.clara.net
email. d.beaumont@cableinet.co.uk
Tackling desertification in Tanzania. No
volunteers needed at the moment.

SUNSEED TRUST (UK CONTACT)
Eastside, Huntingdon PE18 7BY.
Tel/Fax. 01480 411784.
Website. www.sunseed.clara.net
email. sunseed@clara.net
Spanish based project – volunteers
needed.

SUSTAIN – THE ALLIANCE FOR BETTER
FOOD AND FARMING
94 White Lion Street,
London N1 9PF.
Website.
www.users.charity.vfree.com/s/sustain
A coalition of charities and food
producers.

THE SOIL ASSOCIATION
Bristol House, 40-56 Victoria Street,
Bristol BS1 6BY.
Tel. 0117 929 0661   **Fax.** 0117 925 2504.
Website. www.soilassociation.org
email. info@soilassociation.org
The organic growers organisation in the
UK.

THE VEGAN ORGANIC NETWORK
Anandavan, 58 High Lane,
Chorlton-cum-Hardy,
Manchester M21 9DZ.
Tel. 0161 860 4869.
Website. www.veganvillage.co.uk
email. vohan@net-work.co.uk
Go organic without animal manure.

WILLING WORKERS ON
ORGANIC FARMS (WWOOF)
Main Office, PO BOX 2675,
Lewes, East Sussex BN7 1RB.
Tel/Fax. 01273 476 286.
Website. www.phdcc.com/wwoof
email. wwoof-uk@freeserve.com.uk
Matches volunteers with organic farmers.

Books

ORGANIC FARMING
Nicholas Lampkin,
Farming Press, 1990, 720pp, £21.95.
An indispensible text book.

THE ORGANIC GARDEN BOOK
Geoff Hamilton, Dorling Kindersley,
1987, 288pp, £14.99.
If you need a good introduction this is a
fine book.

Magazines

LIVING EARTH
Bristol House,
40-56 Victoria Street, Bristol BS1 6BY.
Tel. 0117 929 0661   **Fax.** 0117 925 2504.
Website. www.soilassociation.org

email. info@soilassociation.org
News and features for organic farmers.

ORGANIC GARDENING
PO Box 29, Minehead,
Somerset TA24 6YY.
Tel/Fax. 01984 641212.
Monthly mag. for organic gardeners.

PERMACULTURE
Hyden House Ltd, The Sustainability
Centre, East Meon, Hampshire GU32
1HR.
Tel. 01730 823311   **Fax.** 01730 823322.
Website. www.permaculture.co.uk
email. help@permaculture.co.uk
Packed with contacts, courses and
opportunities.

THE ORGANIC WAY
HDRA, Ryton Organic Gardens,
Coventry CV8 3LG.
Tel. 024 7630 8215   **Fax.** 024 7630 9229.
Website. www.hdra.org.uk
email. enquiry@hdra.org.uk
Quarterly magazine of the HDRA – very
useful.

Transport

Organisations

CAR SHARING
International Ecotechnology Research Centre, Cranfield University, Cranfield, Bedford MK43 0AL.
Tel. 01234 754097.
Research about car sharing.

ENVIRONMENTAL TRANSPORT ASSOCIATION (ETA)
10 Church Street, Weybridge KT13 8RS.
Tel. 01932 828882.
Website. www.eta.co.uk

SUSTRANS
35 King Street, Bristol BS1 4DZ.
Tel. 0117 9268 893.
Website. www.sustrans.org.uk

THE COMMUNITY TRANSPORT ASSOCIATION
Highbank, Halton Street,
Hyde, Cheshire SK14 2NY.
Tel. 0161 367 8780.
Website.
www.dfpace.dial.pipex.com/cta.man

TRANSPORT 2000
Impact Centre,
12-18 Hoxton Street, London N1 6NG.
Tel. 020 7613 0743.

Books

ENCYCLOPEDIA
Various authors, Open Road,
Annual, 144pp, £12.00.
The guide to alternatives in cycling.

FROM THE FRYER TO THE FUEL TANK: THE COMPLETE GUIDE TO USING VEGETABLE OIL AS AN ALTERNATIVE FUEL
Joshua and Kaia Tickell,
GreenTeach Publishing, 162pp, £19.95.
Story of the vegetable oil car.

General –
Business and innovation

Organisations

BRITISH ASSOCIATION
OF FAIR TRADE SHOPS
Gateway World Shop, Market Place,
Durham DH1 3NJ.

BUSINESS FOR SOCIAL RESPONSIBILITY
609 Mission Street/Second Floor,
San Francisco, CA 94105 – 3506, USA.
Tel. 001 415 537 0888.
Website. www.bsr.org

BUSINESS LINK
87 offices around the country.
Tel. 0345 567765 (for details of your
nearest branch).
Business advice for staring up.

CENTRE FOR HUMAN ECOLOGY
12 Roseneath Place, Edinburgh EH9 1JB.
Tel. 0131 624 1972.
Website. www.che.ac.uk

CENTRE FOR TOMORROW'S COMPANY
19 Buckingham Street,
London WC2N 6EF.
Tel. 020 7930 5150.
Website. www.tomorrowscompany.com

COALITION FOR ENVIRONMENTALLY
RESPONSIBLE ECONOMICS
11 Arlington Street,
Boston, MA 02116-3411, USA.
Tel. 001 617 247 0700.
Website. www.ceres.org

ENVIRONMENTAL
INDUSTRIES COMMISSION
45 Weymouth Street, London W1N 3LD.
Tel. 0207 935 1675.
Website. www.eic-uk.co.uk

ETHICAL TRADING INITIATIVE
16 Baldwin Gardens,
S. 204, London EC1N 7RJ.
Tel. 020 7242 0515.
Website. www.ethicaltrade.org

FEDERATION OF SMALL BUSINESSES
Whittle Way, Blackpool Business Park,
Blackpool, Lancashire FY4 2FE.
Tel. 01253 336000.
Website. www.fsb.org.uk

FORUM FOR THE FUTURE
227a City Road, London EC1V 1JT.
Tel. 020 7251 6070/020 7477 7720
(Scholarships).
Website. www.forumforthefuture.org.uk
Good scholarship scheme available.

GRADUATE ENTERPRISE (SCOTLAND)
Graduate Enterprise Programme,
Careers Service, University of Stirling,
Stirling FK9 4LA.
Tel. 01786 473171.
Offer briefing seminars on starting up in
Scotland.

HIGHLANDS AND ISLANDS ENTERPRISE
Bridge House, 20 Bridge Street,
Inverness IV1 1QR.
Tel. 01463 234171.
Website. www.hie.co.uk
Encourages new business.

INSTITUTE FOR SOCIAL INVENTIONS
20 Heber Road, London NW2 6AA.
Tel. 020 8208 2853   **Fax.** 020 8452 6434.
Website. www.globalideasbank.org
email. rhino@dial.pipex.com
Promotes social innovations.

LEDU
LEDU House, Upper Galwally,
Belfast BT8 6TB.
Tel. 028 90491031   **Fax.** 028 90691432.
Website. www.ledu-ni.gov.uk
Helps small firms in Northern Ireland.

NEW ACADEMY OF BUSINESS
17-19 Clare Street, Bristol BS1 1XA.
Tel. 0117 925 2006.
Website. www.new-academy.ac.uk

OUT OF THIS WORLD
106 High Street, Gosforth,
Newcastle Upon Tyne NE3 1HB.
Tel. 0191 213 5377   **Fax.** 0191 213 5378.
Website. www.ootw.co.uk
email. info@ootw.co.uk
Chain of organic shops.

PRINCE OF WALES
BUSINESS LEADERS FORUM
15-16 Cornwall Terrace,
Regent's Park, London NW1 4QP.
Tel. 020 7467 3656.

SCOTTISH ENTERPRISE
120 Bothwell Street, Glasgow G2 7JP.
Tel. 0141 2482700.
Website. www.scotent.co.uk
Encourages new business in Scotland.

SHARED EARTH LTD
1 Minster Gate, York YO1 7HL.
Tel. 01904 431143.
Website. www.sharedearth.co.uk

SHELL LIVEWIRE
Freepost NT805,
Newcastle upon Tyne NE1 1BR.
Tel. 0345 573 252   **Fax.** 0191 261 1910.
Website. www.shell-livewire.co.uk
email. livewire@projectne.co.uk
Business advice and information for start-up.

SOCIAL VENTURE NETWORK EUROPE
4 Great James Street,
London WC1N 3DA.
Tel. 020 7242 4990.
Website. www.svneurope.com

SUSTAINABILITY
49-53 Kensington High Street,
London W8 5ED.
Tel. 020 7937 9996.
Website. www.sustainability.co.uk

THE ASSOCIATION OF
FAIR TRADE SHOPS IN IRELAND
24 Botanic Avenue, Belfast BT7 1JQ.

THE BODY SHOP INTERNATIONAL PLC
Watersmead, Littlehampton,
West Sussex BN17 6LS.
Tel. 01903 731500   **Fax.** 01903 726250.
Website. www.uk.the-body-shop.com
High street store with green reputation.

THE NATURAL STEP UK
9 Imperial Square, Cheltenham GL50
1QB.
Tel. 01242 262 744.
Website. www.naturalstep.org

THE PRINCES TRUST
(See Grants and Loans).
Start-up grants and loans for small
business.

THE WELSH DEVELOPMENT AGENCY
Principality House,
The Friary, Cardiff CF10 3FE.
Tel. 0845 7775577.
Website. www.wda.co.uk
Encourages new business in Wales.

TRAINING AND EMPLOYMENT AGENCY
Adelaide house, 39/49 Adelaide Street ,
Belfast BT2 8FD.
Tel. 028 90257777.
Website. www.tea-ni.org
Encourages business in Northern Ireland.

UNIT FOR DEVELOPMENT
OF ALTERNATIVE PRODUCTS
Coventry University,
Priory Street, Coventry CV1 5FB.
Tel. 024 76 838816   **Fax.** 024 76 838508.
Assist in product development and
marketing.

UNIVERSITY OF STIRLING
The Administrator, MSc in Entreprenurial
Studies, University of Stirling,
Stirling FK9 4LA.
Tel. 01786 467347.
One year course in being an entrepreneur.

WORLD BUSINESS COUNCIL FOR
SUSTAINABLE DEVELOPMENT
160 Route de Florissant,
CH-1231 Conches, Switzerland.
Tel. 41 22 839 3100.
Website. www.wbcsd.ch

WORLD RESOURCES INSTITUTE
1709 New York Avenue,
Washington DC, 20006, USA.
Website. www.wri.org

YELLOW PAGES ON ENVIRONMENTALLY
SOUND TECHNOLOGIES
UN Environment Programme.
Tel. 00 33 1 4437 1450.

Books

MID-COURSE CORRECTION
Ray C Anderson, Chelsea Green
(available from Green Books in UK),
1999, 204pp, £12.95.
Billed as "required reading for every CEO
in the world".

NATURAL CAPITALISM:
THE NEXT INDUSTRIAL REVOLUTION
Hawken, Lovins and Lovins,
Chelsea Green, 1999, 396pp, £18.99.
A major contribution to economic thinking.

Magazines

ETHICAL CONSUMER
ECRA Publishing Ltd, UNit 21,
41 Old Birlwey Street,
Manchester M15 5RF.
Tel. 0161 226 2929 **Fax.** 0161 226 6277.
Website. www.ethicalconsumer.org
email. ethicon@mcr1.poptel.org.uk
Find out which companies are ethical.

GREEN FUTURES (SUBSCRIPTIONS)
Circa, 13-17 Sturton Street,
Cambridge CB1 2SN.
Tel. 01223 568017 **Fax.** 01223 354643.
email. greenfutures@circa-
uk.demon.co.uk
Positive solutions for sustainable
development.

Careers help

Organisations

BUSINESS AND TECHNOLOGY EDUCATION COUNCIL
Edexcel, Stewart House,
32 Russell Square, London WC1B 5DN.
Tel. 020 7416 8400   **Fax.** 020 7393 4445.
Website. www.edexcel.org.uk
Details of qualifications.

CAREERS RESEARCH AND ADVISORY COUNCIL
Sheraton House, Castle Park,
Cambridge CB3 0AX.
Tel. 01223 460277   **Fax.** 01223 311708.
Website. www.crac.org.uk/crac
email. enquiries@CRAC.org.uk
Publish careers booklets.

CAREERS SUPPORT UNIT
Prospects House, Booth Street East,
Manchester M13 9EP.
Tel. 0161 277 5240   **Fax.** 0161 277 5250.
List published in their free booklet
Administration and Public Sector Management.

DEPARTMENT FOR EDUCATION AND EMPLOYMENT (DfEE)
Sanctuary Buildings,
Great Smith Street, London SW1 3BT.
Tel. 020 7925 5000   **Fax.** 020 7925 6000.
Publishes several useful booklets (see books).

DEPARTMENT OF INTERNATIONAL DEVELOPMENT
94 Victoria Street London SW1E 5JL.
Tel. 020 7917 7000   **Fax.** 020 7917 0016.
Website. www.dfid.gov.uk
Produces booklets about working abroad.

EDEXCEL FOUNDATION
Stewart House,
32 Russel Square, London WC1B 5DN.
Tel: 020 7393 4444   **Fax.** 020 7393 4445.
Website. www.edexcel
email. enquiries@edexcel.org.uk
Information about NVQs and GNVQs.

EDUCATIONAL COUNSELLING AND CREDIT TRANSFER INFORMATION SERVICE
ECTIS 2000 Ltd, Oriel House, Oriel Road,
Cheltenham, Glouscstershire GL50 1XP.
Tel. 01242 252 627   **Fax.** 01242 258 600.
Website. www.ectis.co.uk
Computer access to information on 100,000 courses.

SCOTTISH QUALIFICATIONS AUTHORITY
Hanover House,
24 Douglas Street, Glasgow G2 7NQ.
Tel. 0141 248 7900   **Fax.** 0141 242 2244.
Details of all qualifications in Scotland.

SHELL STEP
Tel. 01623 469030.
Website. www.shell-step.org.uk
Helps secure work experience projects.

THE NATIONAL CENTRE FOR WORK EXPERIENCE
344-354 Grays Inn Road,
London WC1X 8BP.
Tel. 020 7833 9723.
Website. www.ncwe.com
email. ncwe@ncwe.com
Support for people who want work experience.

Books

COLLEGES AND UNIVERSITIES IN THE
USA – THE COMPLETE GUIDE FOR
INTERNATIONAL STUDENTS.
Peterson, Vacation Work,
Annual, 1,068 pp, £15.95.
Essential reading if you want to study in
the US.

ENVIRONMENTAL CAREERS HANDBOOK
Institute of Environmental Sciences,
Trotman and Company Ltd,
2000, 200pp, £9.95.
General environmental careers book.

FINANCIAL SUPPORT FOR STUDENTS
DfEE, DfEE, Annual, 44pp, Free.
A guide for those starting in higher
education.

FINANCIAL SUPPORT FOR STUDENTS
DfEE, DfEE, Annual, 44pp, Free.
A guide for those starting in higher
education.

GRADUATE CAREERS
INFORMATION SERIES
Association of Graduate Careers Advisory
Services, Careers Support Unit (CSU),
Annual, 40pp or less, Free.
Excellent general guides to many careers.
Careers libraries should stock the whole
series.

GREEN VOLUNTEERS – THE WORLD
GUIDE TO VOLUNTARY WORK IN
NATURE CONSERVATION
Green Volunteers, Vacation Work
Publications, 1999, 272pp, £10.99.
Guide to worldwide voluntary
opportunities.

INTERNATIONAL DIRECTORY OF
VOLUNTARY WORK
Various authors, Vacation Work,
1997, 287pp, £9.99.
It is as the title suggests a volunteer's
directory.

JUST THE JOB
Employment Service,
DfEE, Annual, 48pp, Free.
A guide to what your job centre can do for
you.

POSTGRAD: THE DIRECTORY OF
GRADUATE STUDIES
Various authors, Hobsons, Annual,
Page length varies, Price not available.
Over 20,000 postgraduate qualifications
listed.

PROSPECTS POSTGRADUATE
FUNDING GUIDE
AGCAS, Careers Support Unit,
Annual, 36pp, Free.
Funding opportunities for postgraduates.

TAKING A GAP YEAR
Susan Griffith, Vacation Work,
1999, 320pp, £11.95.
A good handbook if you want a year off.

THE DIRECTORY OF
SUMMER JOBS IN BRITAIN 2000
David Woodworth, Vacation Work,
1999, 272 pp, £9.99.
30,000 vacancies listed – some should be
of use.

THE ENVIRONMENTAL FUNDING GUIDE
Susan Forrester and David Caffon,
The Directory of Social Change,
1998, 432pp, £16.95.
Covers all the major sources of funding.

WORKING WITH THE ENVIRONMENT
Tim Ryder, Vacation Work,
2000, 272pp, £11.95.
General environmental careers book.

WORLDWIDE VOLUNTEERING
FOR YOUNG PEOPLE
Various authors, How to Books,
1999, 485pp, £15.95.
General guide to volunteer organisations.

YOUR ULTIMATE CAREER GUIDE
AGCAS, Hobsons, Annual,
1000+pp, Price varies.
Graduate careers and recruitment
directory.

Magazines

CAREER
On Course Publications,
121 King Street, London W6 9JG.
Tel. 020 8600 5300   **Fax.** 020 8741 7716.
Website. www.givemeajob.co.uk
Graduate careers magazine with chapter
on eco-jobs.

CAREER SCOPE
12A Princes Way,
Camberley, Surrey GU15 3SP.
Tel. 01276 21188   **Fax.** 01276 91833.
Website. www.isco.org.uk
email. info@isco.org.uk
General careers magazine with useful
features.

ENVIRONMENT POST
c/o Pathway UK Ltd, PO Box 5903,
Basildon, Essex SS12 0YZ.
Tel. 01268 468000.
Website. www.environmentpost.co.uk
Monthly with job adverts.

NEW SCIENTIST
151 Wardour Street, London W1V 4BN.
Tel. 020 7331 2701   **Fax.** 020 7331 2777.
Website. www.newscientist.com
Scientific vacancies every week.

OCCUPATIONS
COIC, PO Box 298a,
Thames Ditton, Surrey KT2 0ZS.
Tel. 020 8957 5030   **Fax.** 020 8957 5019.
General careers information.

PROSPECTS TODAY
CSU Ltd, Prospects House,
Booth Street East, Manchester M13 9EP.
Tel. 0161 277 5200   **Fax.** 0161 277 5210.
Graduate vacancies weekly.

Environmental

Organisations

BLACK ENVIRONMENT NETWORK
9 Llainwen Uchaf,
Llanberis, Gwynedd LL55 4LL.
Tel. 01286 870 715.

CENTRES FOR CHANGE
c/o Friends Meeting House,
43 St. Giles, Oxford OX1 3LW.
Tel. 01865 316338 **Fax.** 01865 516288.
Website. www.oneworld.org/brightpeace
email. cfc@centres.demon.co.uk
UK network of environmental centres.

ENVIRONMENTAL INFORMATION
SERVICE
PO Box 197, Cawston,
Norwich, Norfolk NR10 4BH.
Tel/Fax. 01603 871048.
Website. www.benefits.co.uk/eis
email. information@eisuk.demon.co.uk
Link employers and employees – 8000
database.

NORTHERN IRELAND
ENVIRONMENTAL LINK
77 Botanic Avenue, Belfast BT7 1JL.
Tel. 028 90314944.

STUDENTFORCE FOR SUSTAINABILITY
Brewery House, High Street,
Ketton, Stamford PE9 3TA.
Tel. 01780 722072.
Website.
www.ourworld.compuserve.com/
homepages/studentforce/
General information for students.

THE ENVIRONMENT COUNCIL
212 High Holborn, London WC1V 7VW.
Tel. 020 7836 2626 **Fax.** 020 7242 1180.
Website. www.greenchannel.com/tec
email. info@envcouncil.org.uk
Publishes the useful *Habitat* magazine.

Books

MANUAL 2000
Elkington and Hailes,
Hodder and Stoughton,
1999, 420pp, £9.99.
All the major environmental solutions
summed up.

SMALL IS BEAUTIFUL
E.F.Schumacher, Virago,
1973, 259pp, £6.99.
A classic text. Daunting but well worth
reading.

Magazines

CLEAN SLATE
CAT, Machynlleth, Powys SY20 9AZ.
Tel. 01654 702400 **Fax.** 01654 702782.
Website. www.cat.org.uk
email. info@cat.org.uk
News and practical features.

CORPORATE WATCH
Box E, 111 Magdalen Road,
Oxford OX4 1RQ.
Tel/Fax. 01865 791391.
Website. www.oneworld.org/cw
email. Mail@corporate watch.i-way.co.uk
Watching big business for you.

ENDS REPORT
Finsbury Business Centre,
40 Bowling Lane, London EC1R 0NE.
Tel. 020 7814 5300 **Fax.** 020 7415 0106.
Website. www.ends.co.uk
email. post@ends.co.uk
Pricey but lists appointments and
conferences.

ETHICAL CONSUMER
ECRA Publishing Ltd, Unit 21, 41 Old
Birlwey Street, Manchester M15 5RF.
Tel. 0161 226 2929 **Fax.** 0161 226 6277.
Website. www.ethicalconsumer.org
email. ethicon@mcr1.poptel.org.uk
Find out which companies are ethical.

GOING FOR GREEN
Elizabeth House,
The Pier, Wigan WN3 4EX.

GREEN FUTURES
Unit 55, 50-56 Wharf Road,
London N1 7SF.
Tel. 020 7608 2332 **Fax.** 020 7608 2333.
email. post@greenfutures.org.uk
Positive solutions for sustainable
development.

NEW INTERNATIONALIST
Tower House, Lathkill Street,
Market Harborough LE16 9EF.
Tel. 01858 439616 **Fax.** 01858 434958.
Website. www.newint.org
email. ni@newint.org
A different issue each month –
development bias.

PEOPLE AND THE PLANET
Suite 112, Spitfire Studios, 63-71 Collier
Street, London N1 9BE.
Tel. 020 7713 8108 **Fax.** 020 7713 8109.
Website. www.oneworld.org/patp
email. planet21@netcomuk.co.uk
Positive and easy to read – a good source
of information.

POSITIVE NEWS
The Six Bells, Church Street,
Bishops Castle, Shropshire SY9 5AA.
Tel. 01588 630121 **Fax.** 01588 630122.
Website.
www.oneworld.org/positive_news
email. positive.news@btineternet.com
Antidote to depressing news stories –
informs.

THE ECOLOGIST
c/o Cissbury House, Furze View, Five
Oaks Road, Sinfold, West Sussex, RH13
7RH.
Tel. 01403 786726 **Fax.** 01403 782644.
email. sgc@mag-subs.demon.co.uk
In-depth and radical – not for the faint
hearted.

THE GREEN GUIDE
271 Upper Street,
Islington, London N1 2UQ.
Tel. 020 7345 2709 **Fax.** 020 7226 1311.
Website. www.greenguide.co.uk

Grants and loans

Organisations

ASSOCIATION OF BRITISH CREDIT UNIONS
(See Alternatives).
Credit unions make small loans for enterprises.

ASSOCIATION OF COMMUNITY TRUSTS AND FOUNDATIONS
4 Bloomsbury Square, London WC1A 2RL.
Tel. 020 7831 0033.

ASSOCIATION OF MBAS
(MASTER OF BUSINESS ADMINISTRATION)
15 Duncan Terrace, London N1 8BZ.
Tel. 020 7837 3375   **Fax.** 020 7278 3634.
Website. www.mba.org.uk
email. c.oldacre@mba.org.uk
Students borrow up to two-thirds of their pre-course salary plus tuition fees for each year of full time study.

ASTON REINVESTMENT TRUST
The Rectory, 3 Tower Street,
Birmingham B19 3UY.
Tel. 0121 359 2444.
Website. www.arq.co.uk/art
Encourages self-reliance in high risk areas.

BIOTECHNOLOGY AND BIOLOGICAL SCIENCES RESEARCH COUNCIL (BBSRC)
Polaris House, North Star Avenue,
Swindon SN2 1UH.
Tel. 01793 413200   **Fax.** 01793 413201.
Website. www.bbsrc.ac.uk
Grant making body for postgraduates.

BRITISH FEDERATION OF WOMEN GRADUATES
4 Mandeville Courtyard, 142 Battersea Park Road, London SW11 4NB.
Tel. 020 7498 8037   **Fax.** 020 7498 8037.
Scholarships for postgraduate research for women.

CAREER DEVELOPMENT LOANS
Tel. 0800 585505.
CDLs between £300 and £8,000 are made by participating banks and the DfEE. Repayment starts a month after graduation.

DEPARTMENT FOR EDUCATION AND EMPLOYMENT
Mowden Hall, Staindrop Road,
Darlington, County Durham DL3 9BG.
Tel. 0800 731 9133
or textphone 0800 210 280.
Website. www.dfee.gov.uk
Information on funding, including the Disabled Students Allowance.

DEPARTMENT OF EDUCATION FOR NORTHERN IRELAND
Rathgael House, Balloo Road,
Bangor, County Down BT19 7PR.
Tel. 028 91279279   **Fax.** 028 91279100.
Advice for students.

ECOLOGY BUILDING SOCIETY
Freepost, 18 Station Road,
Cross Hills, Keighley BD20 5BR.
Tel. 0845 674 5566.
Website. www.ecology.co.uk
Gives loans to eco-business and homes.

ECONOMIC AND SOCIAL RESEARCH COUNCIL
Polaris House,
North Star Avenue, Swindon SN2 1UJ.

Tel. 01793 413043   **Fax.** 01793 413056.
Website. www.esrc.ac.uk
Grant making body for postgraduates.

EDUCATIONAL GRANT ADVISORY
SERVICE
501-505 Kingsland Road,
Dalston, London E8 4AU.
Tel. 020 7249 6636.
Independent advisory agency for people
wanting to get funding for further and
higher education.

ENGINEERING AND PHYSICAL
RESEARCH COUNCIL
Polaris House, North Star Avenue,
Swindon SN2 1ET.
Tel. 01793 444000   **Fax.** 01793 444012.
Website. www.epsrc.ac.uk
Grant making body for postgraduates.

ENGLISH PARTNERSHIPS
COMMUNITY INVESTMENT FUND
16-18 Old Queen St., London SW1H 9HP.
Tel. 020 7976 7070   **Fax.** 020 7976 7740.
Website. www.englishpartnerships.co.uk
Grants between £10,000 - £100,000.

ENVIRONMENT WALES
4th Floor, Empire House,
Mount Stuart Square, Cardiff CF1 6DN.
Tel. 029 2049 5737.
email. lynowen@princes-trust.org.uk
Issues start up grants to projects in
Wales.

ETHICAL INVESTMENT
RESEARCH SERVICE (EIRIS)
80-84 Bondway, London SW8 1SF.
Tel. 0207 840 5700   **Fax.** 0207 735 5323.
Website. www.eiris.u-net.com
Helps you find out about ethical funds.

ICOF COMMUNITY CAPITAL
12-14 Gold Street, Northampton NN1 1RS.
Tel. 01604 37563   **Fax.** 01604 36165.
Lends to worker co-ops and social
business.

INSTITUTION OF ELECTRICAL ENGINEERS
Savoy Place, London WC2R OBL.
Tel. 020 7240 1871   **Fax.** 020 7497 3609.
Website. www.iee.org.uk
email. scholarships@iee.org.uk
Awards some grants for postgraduates.

LOCAL INVESTMENT FUND
Business in the Community,

44 Baker Street, London W1M 1DH.
Tel. 020 7224 1600   **Fax.** 020 7486 1700.
Loans for urban community projects –
£25,000 - £250,000.

MEDICAL RESEARCH COUNCIL (MRC)
20 Park Crescent, London W1N 4AL.
Tel. 020 7636 5422   **Fax.** 020 7637 0361.
Website. www.mrc.ac.uk
Grant making body for postgraduates.

NATIONAL BUREAU FOR
STUDENTS WITH DISABILITIES
4th Floor, Chapter House,
Crucifix Lane, London SE1 3JW.
Tel. 020 7450 0620 (voice/minicom).
Advice on applying for grants.

NATIONAL UNION OF STUDENTS
The Welfare Unit, NUS,
461 Holloway Road, London N7 6LJ.
Provides information sheets on student
finance.

PARTICLE PHYSICS AND
ASTRONOMY RESEARCH COUNCIL
Polaris House, North Star Avenue,
Swindon SN2 1SZ.
Tel. 01793 442000.
Website. www.pparc.ac.uk
Grant making body for postgraduates.

PROSPECTS
Careers Services Unit, Prospect House,
Booth Street East, Manchester M13 9EP.
Tel. 0161 277 5200   **Fax.** 0161 277 5220.
Website. www.prospects.csu.ac.uk
Excellent web site and publications with
more grants listed.

SHELL BETTER BRITAIN CAMPAIGN
King Edward House,
135a New Street, Birmingham B2 4QA.
Tel. 0121 2485900   **Fax.** 0121 2485901.
Website. www.sbbc.co.uk
email. enquiries@sbbc.co.uk
Free magazine with potential funding
sources.

STUDENT AWARDS AGENCY
FOR SCOTLAND
Gyleview House, 3 Redheughs Rigg,
South Gyle, Edinburgh EH12 9HH.
Tel. 0131 476 8212   **Fax.** 0131 244 5887.
Advice for students.

STUDENT LOANS COMPANY LIMITED
100 Bothwell Street, Glasgow G2 7JD.

Tel. 0800 405 010.
Main loan making body for students.

THE BRITISH ACADEMY
Arts and Humanities Research Board, 10
Carlton House Terrace,
London, SW1Y 5AH.
Tel. 020 7969 5200   **Fax.** 020 7969 5300.
Website. www.britac3.britac.ac.uk
Grant making body for postgraduates.

THE DIRECTORY OF SOCIAL CHANGE
24 Stephenson Way, London NW1 2DP.
Tel. 020 7209 5151.
Publishes   .

THE PRINCE'S YOUTH BUSINESS TRUST
PYBT Head Office,
5 Cleveland Place, London SW1Y 6JJ.
Tel. 020 7925 2900.
Offers average loan or grant of £2,500.

THE SOCIAL INVESTMENT FUND
Charities Aid Foundation,
Kings Hill, West Malling, Kent ME19 4TA.
Tel. 01732 520000   **Fax.** 01732 520001.
Website. www.cafonline.org
Gives affordable loans to charities.

TRIODOS BANK
Brunel House, 11 The Promenade,
Clifton, Bristol BS8 3NN.
Tel. 0500 008 720.
Website. www.tridos.co.uk
Offers loans for eco-business.

UK SOCIAL INVESTMENT FORUM
Suite 308, 16 Baldwins Gardens,
London EC1N 7PJ.
Tel. 020 7404 1993.
email. www.uksif.org
Publishes list of members active in ethical
investment.

UNITY TRUST BANK PLC
4 The Square, 111 Broad Street,
Birmingham B15 1AR.
Tel. 0121 616 4146.
Website. www.unitygroup.co.uk
Offers loans.

WELSH OFFICE EDUCATION
DEPARTMENT
FHE1 Division, 4th Floor,
Cathays Park, Cardiff CF1 3NQ.
Tel. 029 20825831   **Fax.** 029 20825823.
Advice for students.

Books

A GUIDE TO THE MAJOR TRUSTS, VOL 1&II
Fitzherbert, Addison & Rahman, The
Directory of Social Change, Annual,
1998, 382pp, £19.95 (each volume).
Useful for charities looking for funding.

FINANCIAL SUPPORT FOR STUDENTS
DfEE, DfEE, Annual, 44pp, Free.
A guide for those starting in higher
education.

PROSPECTS POSTGRADUATE
FUNDING GUIDE
AGCAS, Careers Support Unit,
Annual, 36pp, Free.
Funding opportunities for postgraduates.

THE ENVIRONMENTAL FUNDING GUIDE
Susan Forrester and David Caffon,
The Directory of Social Change,
1998, 432pp, £16.95.
Covers all the major sources of funding.

Mail order book companies

Organisations

CENTRAL BUREAU FOR EDUCATIONAL
VISITS AND EXCHANGES
10 Spring Gardens, London, SW1A 2BN.
Tel. 020 7389 4004   **Fax.** 020 7389 4426.
Website. www.britishcouncil.org/cbeve/
Publishers of vacation, volunteer and
exchange books.

CENTRE FOR ALTERNATIIVE
TECHNOLOGY
Machynlleth, Powys Wales. SY20 9AZ.
Tel. 01654 702400   **Fax.** 01654 702782.
email. info@cat.org.uk
Publishes books, leaflets and resource
guides on sustainable solutions for
domestic, educational and commercial
use.

ECO-LOGIC BOOKS
Mulberry House,
19 Maple Grove, Bath BA2 3AF.
Tel. 01225 484 472   **Fax.** 0117 942 0164.
email. books@eco-logic.demon.co.uk

GAIA BOOKS
66 Charlotte Street, London W1P 1LR.
Tel. 020 7323 4010   **Fax.** 020 7323 0435.
Publishes illustrated reference books.

GREEN BOOKS
Foxhole, Dartington,
Totnes, Devon TQ9 6EB.
Tel/Fax. 01803 863260.
Website. www.greenbooks.co.uk
email. greenbooks@gn.apc.org
Imports many fine American books.

HDRA
(See Organic Growing).

HOBSONS
The Distribution Department, Hobsons
Publishing PLC, 159-173 St John Street,
London EC1V 4DR.
Website. www.hobsons.co.uk
Britain's biggest careers publisher.

JON CARPENTER
2 Home Farm Cottage, Sandy Lane,
St Paul's Cray, Kent, BR5 3HZ.
Tel. 01689 870437.
Interesting range of books, including
vegan titles.

KOGAN PAGE/EARTHSCAN
120 Pentonville Road, London N1 9JN.
Tel. 020 7278 0433   **Fax.** 020 7837 6348.
Website. www.earthscan.co.uk
email. kpinfo@kogan-page.co.uk
Selection of general careers and eco
titles.

NATURAL HISTORY BOOK SERVICE
2-3 Willis Road, Totnes, Devon TQ9 5XN.
Tel. 01803 865913   **Fax.** 01803 865280.
Website. www.nhbs.com
email. nhbs@nhbs.co.uk
Massive selection of titles on a wide range
of subjects.

PERMANENT PUBLICATIONS
The Sustainability Centre,
East Meon, Hampshire GU32 1HR.
Tel. 01730 823311   **Fax.** 01730 823322.
Website. www.permaculture.co.uk
email. hello@permaculture.co.uk

TROTMANS PUBLISHING
2 The Green, Richmond, Surrey TW9 1PL.
Tel. 020 8486 1150   **Fax.** 020 8486 1151.

Website. www.trotman.co.uk
Publishes a range of useful publications.

VACATION WORK PUBLICATIONS
9 Park End Street, Oxford OX11 1HJ.
Tel. 01865 241978   **Fax.** 01865 790885.
Website. www.vacationwork.co.uk
email. sales@vacationwork.co.uk
Books on voluntary work and summer
jobs.

BROADLEYS PUBLISHING
Buriton House, Station Road, Newport,
Saffron Waldon, Essex CB11 3PL.
Tel. 01799 540922   **Fax.** 01799 541367.
Website. www.mistral.co.uk/cgs
email. cgs.broadleys.com
Smallholding books and magazine.

INTERMEDIATE TECHNOLOGY
PUBLICATIONS
103-105 Southampton Row,
London WC1B 4HH.
Tel. 020 7436 9761   **Fax.** 020 7436 2013.
Website.
www.oneworld.org/itdg/publications
email. orders@itpubs.org.uk
Biggest UK supplier of development
books.

Places to visit

BATH ENVIRONMENT CENTRE
24 Millsom Street,
Bath, Somerset BA1 1DG.
Tel. 01225 460620 **Fax.** 01225 460840.
Website.
web.ukonline.co.uk/bath.environmental
email. bath.environment@ukonline.co.uk
Eco-visitor centre.

BISHOPS WOOD ENVIRONMENTAL
EDUCATION CENTRE
Crossway Green, Stourport-on-Severn,
Worcs. DY13 9SE.
Tel. 01299 250513 **Fax.** 01299 250131.
Website.
www.4seasons.org.uk/centres/bishop
email. bishopswood@4seasons.org.uk
Eco-visitor centre.

CENTRE FOR ALTERNATIVE
TECHNOLOGY
Europe's leading eco visitor centre.
(See p.148 for details).

EARTH BALANCE
West Sleekburn Farm, Bomarsund,
Bedlington, Northumberland NE22 7AD.
Tel. 01670 821000 **Fax.** 01670 821026.
Website. www.earth-balance.co.uk
email. info@earth-balance.co.uk
Eco visitor centre. Open all year.

EARTH CENTRE
Denaby Main, Doncaster,
South Yorkshire DN12 4EA.
Tel. 01709 512000 **Fax.** 01709 512010.
Multimillion pound millenium project. Not
open yet – contact before visiting.

ECOLOGICAL VILLAGE PROJECT
Findhorn Foundation, The Park,

Forres, Scotland IV36 0TZ.
Tel. 01309 690154 **Fax.** 01309 691387.
Website. www.findhorn.org
email. ecovillage@findhorn.org.internet
Twenty eco houses; also spiritual retreats.

ECOTECH CENTRE
Castle Acre Road,
Swaffham, Norfolk PE37 7HT.
Tel. 01760 726 100 **Fax.** 01760 726 109.
Eco-visitor centre.

ENERGY 21 RENEWABLE ENERGY PARK
PO Box 154, Stroud,
Gloucestershire GL5 3YU.
Tel. 01453 752 277 **Fax.** 01453 752 244.
Website. www.energy21.org.uk
email. info@energy21.org.uk
Proposes renewable energy park.

HENRY DOUBLEDAY RESEARCH
ASSOCIATION (HDRA)
(See Organic Growing).

HOCKERTON HOUSING PROJECT
2 Mystery Hill, Gables Drive, Hockerton,
Southwell, Nottinghamshire, NG25 0QU.
Tel. 01636 816902.;
email. nwhite@fatmac.demon.co.uk
Eco-homes tour available on request (fee).

MIDDLEWOOD TRUST
Middle Wood, Roeburndale West,
Lancaster, Lancashire LA2 8QX.
Tel. 01524 221880.
email. middlewood@lancs.ac.uk
Courses and voluntary work available.

NATURAL SURROUNDINGS
CENTRE FOR WILDLIFE GARDENING
Bayfield Estate, Holt, Norfolk NR25 7JN.

Tel. 01263 711091.
Gardening display centre.

PLANTS FOR A FUTURE
(See Organic Growing).

SHERWOOD ENERGY VILLAGE
Sherwood Lodge, Annexe, Sherwood
Drive, New Ollerton, Nottinghamshire
NG22 9PP.
Tel/Fax. 01263 863887.
email. sev@netcomuk.co.uk
Proposed eco-demonstration park.

SONAIRTE
The Ninch, Laytown,
County Meath, Ireland.
Tel. +353 41 27572 **Fax.** +353 41 28130.
email. sonairte@drogheda.edunet.ie
Alternative energy centre.

THE ECO CENTRE
Windmill Way, Hebburn,
Tyne and Wear NE31 1SR.
Tel. 0191 428 1144 **Fax.** 0191 428 1155.
email. south.tyneside@groundwork.org.uk
Commercial building with eco-
technologies.

THE ECO-HOUSE
Western Park, Hinkley Road,
Leicester, Leicestershire LE3 6HX.
Tel. 0116 222 0239 **Fax.** 0116 255
2343.
Website. www.environ.org.uk
email. ben@environ.org.uk
Environmental show home.

THE GREENHOUSE ENERGY CENTRE
35 Mill Street, St Peter Port, Guernsey,
Channel Islands GY1 1HG.
Tel. 01481 722299 **Fax.** 01481 723200.
Website. www.begin666.com
email. energyservices@begin666.com
Ecology and fair trade centre.

WOODLAND FUN SHOW
c/o Birchall Cottage, Copt Oak,
Markfield, Leicestershire LE67 9QD.
Tel. 01530 243 904.
Based in 30 acre wood, powered by
renewables.

Positive economics and alternative work styles

Organisations

ACRE (ACTION WITH COMMUNITIES IN RURAL ENGLAND)
Somerford Court, Somerford Road,
Cirencester, Gloucestershire GL7 1TW.
Tel. 01285 653477   **Fax.** 01285 654537.
Supports small rural businesses.

ASSET DEMOCRACY
The Old School, 29 Bailbrook Lane,
Swainswick, Bath BA1 7AN.
Tel. 01225 333688.

ASSOCIATION OF BRITISH
CREDIT UNIONS LIMITED (ABCUL)
Holyoake House, Hanover Street,
Manchester M60 0AS.
Tel. 0161 832 3694.
Website. www.abcul.org
Information on starting credit unions.

ASSOCIATION OF COMMUNITY
TRUSTS AND FOUNDATIONS
2 Plough Yard, Shoreditch High Street,
London EC2 3LP.
Tel. 020 7422 8611   **Fax.** 020 7422 8616.
email.
actaf@communityfoundations.org.uk
Helps you set up a community trust.

BRITISH URBAN
REGENERATION ASSOCIATION
33 Great Sutton Street,
London EC1V 0DX.
Tel. 0800 020 8260.
Website.
www.ourworld.compuserve.com/homepag
es/bura

CAMPAIGN FOR COMMUNITY
BANKING SERVICES
50 Roundwood Park,
Harpenden, Herts AL5 3AF.
Tel. 01582 764760.
Website.
www.freeserve.virgin.net/bank.help/service
s.htm

CO-OPERATIVE UNION LTD
Holyoake House, Hanover Street,
Manchester M60 0AS.
Tel. 0161 832 4300   **Fax.** 0161 831 7684.
email. info@co-opunion.org.uk
Co-operative support and advice.

COMMUNES NETWORK
Redfield, Winslow,
Buckinghamshire MK18 3LZ.
Sells *Diggers and Dreamers*; a guidebook
to UK communes.

COMMUNITY ACTION NETWORK
Panton House, 25 Haymarket,
London SW1 4EN.
Tel. 0207 321 224.
Website. www.can-online.org.uk
Gives advice to community groups.

COMMUNITY BUSINESS SCOTLAND
Society Place, West Calder,
West Lothian EH55 8EA.
Tel. 01506 871370.
Supports community enterprise.

COMMUNITY DEVELOPMENT
FOUNDATION
60 Highbury Grove, London N5 2AG.
Tel. 020 7226 5375   **Fax.** 020 7704 0313.
Website. www.cdf.org.uk

email. admin@cdf.org.uk
Useful publications including One Small
Step.

COMMUNITY ENTERPRISE WALES
Community Enterprise House, 36 Union
Terrace, Merthyr Tydfill, Wales CF47 0DY.
Tel. 01685 376 490.

EMPLOYEE OWNERSHIP SCOTLAND
Building 1, Templeton Street,
Bridgton, Glasgow G40 1DA.
Tel. 041 554 3797.

FEDERATION OF SMALL BUSINESSES
347a Garstang Road,
Fulwood, Preston PR2 9UP.
Tel. 01772 712033   **Fax.** 01772 774843.
Operates a credit union.

ICOF COMMUNITY CAPITAL
(See Loans and Grants).
Lends to worker co-ops and social
business.

INDUSTRIAL COMMON
OWNERSHIP FINANCE
115 Hamstead Rd, Handsworth,
Birmingham B20 2BT.
Tel. 0121 523 6886.
email. icom@icom.org.uk
Promotes worker co-ops.

INDUSTRIAL COMMON OWNERSHIP
MOVEMENT (ICOM)
20 Central Road, Leeds LS1 6DE.
Tel. 0113 246 1738.

IRISH LEAGUE OF CREDIT UNIONS
33 Lower Mount Street, Dublin 2, Eire.
Tel. 00 353 1614 6700.
Website. www.creditunion.ie
Gives advice about credit unions.

LETS (LOCAL EXCHANGE
TRADING SCHEMES) LINK
2 Kent Street, Portsea,
Portsmouth, Hants. PO1 3BS.
Tel. 023 92730 639   **Fax.** 023 92730 629.
Website. www.letslinkuk.demon.co.uk
email. lets@letslinkuk.demon.co.uk
Advice on starting or joining a LETS
scheme.

LETS NORTHERN IRELAND
20 Beechwood, Barbridge,
County Down BT32 3YL.
Tel. 028 40623834.

Advice on starting or joining a LETS
scheme.

LETS SOLUTIONS
124 Northmoor Road,
Manchester M12 5RS.
Tel. 0161 224 0749.
For businesses, voluntary organisations
and local authorities.

LETSLINK SCOTLAND
Patrick Boase, 31 Banavie Road,
Glasgow G11 5AW.
Tel. 0141 339 3064.
Advice on starting or joining a LETS
scheme.

NEW ECONOMICS FOUNDATION
Cinnamon House,
6-8 Cole Street, London SE1 4YH.
Tel. 020 7407 7447.
Website. www.neweconomics.org
Information about alternative economics.

NORTHERN IRELAND CO-OPERATIVE
DEVELOPMENT AGENCY
45-49 Donegal Street, Belfast,
Northern Ireland BT1 2FG.
Tel. 028 90232755.
Supports worker co-ops in Northern
Ireland.

RADICAL ROUTES/ROOTSTOCK
28 Hamstead Road, Hockley,
Birmingham B19 1DB.
Tel. 0121 551 1132.
Offers support and finance to co-ops.

SCHOOL FOR SOCIAL ENTREPRENEURS
18 Victoria Park Square, London E2 9FF.
Tel. 020 8983 0300.
Website. www.sse.org.uk
Training and advice given.

SOCIAL ENTERPRISE LONDON
1a Aberdeen Studios,
22-24 Highbury Grove, London N5 2EA.
Tel. 020 7704 7490.
Website. www.sel.org.uk

TEAR FUND
100 Church Road, Teddington,
Middlesex TW11 8QE.
Tel. 020 8977 9144   **Fax.** 020 8943 3594.
Website. www.tearfund.org
Become a volunteer fair trade sales rep.

THE CO-OPERATIVE
DEVELOPMENT AGENCY
Broadmead House, 21 Panton Street,
London SW1Y 4DR.
Tel. 020 7839 2988.

TRAIDCRAFT EXCHANGE
Kingsway, Gateshead,
Tyne and Wear NE11 0NE.
Tel. 0191 491 0591   **Fax.** 0191 482 2690.
Website. www.traidcraft.co.uk
Become a volunteer fair trade sales rep.

UKSIF (SOCIAL INVESTMENT FORUM)
Hollywell Centrer,
No 1 Phipp Street, London EC2A 4PF.
Tel. 020 7749 4880.
Website. www.uksif.org.uk
email. info@uksif.org
Supports ethical investment.

WALES CO-OPERATIVE DEVELOPMENT
AND TRAINING CENTRE (WCDTC)
Llandaff Court, Fairwater Road,
Cardiff CF5 2XP.
Tel. 0222 554955.
Supports co-operatives in Wales.

WELSH DEVELOMENT AGENCY
Community Enterprise Unit,
Business Centre, Triangle Business Park,
Pentrebach, Merthyr Tydfill CF48 4YB.
Tel. 01685 722177.
Supports community enterprise.

Books

ONE SMALL STEP: A GUIDE TO ACTION
ON SUSTAINABLE DEVELOPMENT IN THE
UK
Chris Church and Jan McHarry,
Community Development Fund, 96pp,
£10.95.
Community focused sustainable
development.

SHORT CIRCUIT: STRENGTHENING
LOCAL ECONOMICS FOR SECURITY IN
AN UNSTABLE WORLD
Richard Douthwaite, Green Books,
1998, 400pp, £14.95.
Helps communities to help themselves.

Volunteering

Organisations

**BRITISH VOLUNTEER
AGENCY LIAISON GROUP**
United Nations Association, International
Service, 57 Goodramgate, York, YO1 7FX.
Tel. 01904 647799   **Fax.** 01904 652353.
Website. www.oneworld.org/is
email. unais-uk@geo2.poptel.org.uk
Information about overseeas
opportunities.

**CENTRAL BUREAU FOR EDUCATIONAL
VISITS AND EXCHANGES**
(See Mail Order Book Companies and
Publishers).

COMMUNITY SERVICE VOLUNTEERS
237 Pentonville Road, London N1 9NJ.
Tel. 020 7278 6601   **Fax.** 020 7833 0149.
Website. www.newnet.org.uk/csunat
General information about opportunities.

DIRECTORY OF SOCIAL CHANGE
24 Stephenson Way, London NW1 2DP.
Tel. 020 7209 5151.
Website. www.dsc.org.uk
Produces information on volunteering.

**NATIONAL ASSOCIATION OF
VOLUNTEER BUREAUX**
New Oxford House, Waterloo Street,
Birmingham B2 5UG.
Tel. 0121 633 4555.
Website. www.navb.org.uk
General information about volunteering.

NATIONAL CENTRE FOR VOLUNTEERING
Regents Wharf, 8 All Saints Street,
London N1 9RL.
Tel. 020 7520 8900.
Website. www.volunteering.org.uk
General information about volunteering.

**NATIONAL COALITION
FOR BLACK VOLUNTEERING**
35-37 William Road, London NW1 3ER.
Tel. 020 7387 1681.
Website. www.blink.org.uk/organ/nvbv
Advice for black volunteers.

**NATIONAL COUNCIL FOR
VOLUNTARY ORGANISATIONS**
Regent's Wharf,
All Saints Street, London N1 9RL.
Tel. 020 7713 6161   **Fax.** 020 7713 6300.
Website. www.ncvo-vol.org.uk
Holds information on voluntary
organisations.

**NORTHERN IRELAND VOLUNTEER
DEVELOPMENT AGENCY**
Annsgate House,
70-74 Ann Street, Belfast BT1 4EH.
Tel. 028 90236100.
Encourages volunteering in Northern
Ireland.

RETURNED VOLUNTEER ACTION
1 Amwell Street, London EC1R 1TH.
Tel. 020 7278 0804   **Fax.** 020 7278 7019.
Helps you use overseas experience in the
UK.

VOLPROF
City University Business School,
Frobisher Crescent, Barbican Centre,
London EC2Y 8HB.
Tel. 020 7477 8667.
Centre for voluntary sector and
not-for-profit management.

VOLUNTARY SERVICE OVERSEAS
317 Putney Bridge Road,
Putney, London SW15 2PN.
Tel. 020 8780 2266   **Fax.** 020 8780 1326.
Website. www.vso.org.uk
2 year voluntary placements overseas.

VOLUNTEER DEVELOPMENT SCOTLAND
72 Murray Place, Stirling, FK8 2BX,
Tel. 01786 479593.
Website. www.vds.org.uk
Supports volunteering in Scotland.

WALES COUNCIL FOR VOLUNTARY
ACTION
CYGNAR GWEITHNEDU GWIRFEDDOL
CYMRU LLYSLFOR
Crescent Road, Caerffili,
Mid-Glamorgan CF83 1XL.
Tel. 029 20855100.
Website. www.wcva.org.uk
Supports volunteering in Wales.

Books

(See Careers Help).

Part Four –
Index of organisations

Index of organisations

Business and innovation

Training and Employment Agency
Unit for Development of Alternative Products
University of Stirling
World Business Council for Sustainable Development
World Resources Institute
Yellow Pages on Environmentally Sound Technologies

Campaigning and communication

Animal Aid
British Union for the Abolition of Vivisection
Chartered Institute of Marketing
Earth First!
Ecotrip
Environmental Investigation Agency
Friends of the Earth
Friends of the Earth Scotland
GenetiX Snowball
Greenpeace
Institute of Public Relations
National Council for the Training of Broadcast Journalists
Reclaim the Streets
SchNEWS
The Land is Ours
The Periodicals Training Council
The Women's Environmental Network
Undercurrents
UnderstandingBus
Vegan Society
Veggies

Careers help

Business and Technology Education Council
Careers Research and Advisory Council
Careers Support Unit
Department for Education and Employment (DfEE)

Department of International Development
EDEXCEL Foundation
Educational Counselling and Credit Transfer Information Service
Scottish Qualifications Authority
Shell Step
The National Centre for Work Experience

Conservation

Association of Countryside Rangers
Association of Pole Lathe Turners
Association of National Parks and Countryside Voluntary Wardens
Bioregional Group
British Trust for Conservation Volunteers
Conservation Volunteers Northern Ireland
Countryside Agency
Countryside Commission
Countryside Council for Wales
Countryside Management Association
Earthwatch
English Nature
Forestry Commission Personnel
Future Forests
Groundwork
Institute of Ecology and Environmental Management
International Centre for Conservation Education
Lantra
National Trust
Plantlife
Rainforest Foundation UK
Reforesting Scotland
Royal Society for Nature Conservation and Wildlife Trusts
Royal Society for the Protection of Birds
Scottish Conservation Projects Trust
Scottish Natural Heritage
Scottish Wildlife Trust Ltd

The Dun Beag Project
Trees for Life
Woodland Trust

Construction

Architectural Association
Association for Environment Conscious Building
British Earth Sheltering Association
British Straw Bale Building Association
Building and Social Housing Foundation
Building Research Energy Conservation
Community Self Build Scotland
Construction Industry Environment Forum
Constructive Individuals
Ecological Design Association
Hockerton Housing Project
Royal Institute of British Architects
The Chartered Institute of Building Services
The Community Self Build Agency
The Young Builders Trust
Walter Segal Self Build Trust
Women's Education in Building

Creative arts and design

Arts Council of Great Britain
Arts Council of Northern Ireland
Arts Council of Wales
British Institute of Professional Photography
Britta Boyer
CAPITB Trust
Centre for Sustainable Design
Crafts Council
Design Council
Eco Design
Ecological Design Initiative

Enviro Arts
Green Fibres
Hemp Union
Natural Collection
Platform
Rural Crafts Association
Scottish Arts Council
Scottish Ecological Design Association
Society for Responsible Design
Textile Environment Network
Textile Institute
The Crafts Movement
Virtual Craft Fair

Development
British Council
British Volunteer Agency Liaison Group
Department of International Development
Global Partnership Association
Institute of Development Studies
Intermediate Technology Development Group
Intermediate Technology Publications
Oxfam GB
Powerful Information
Returned Volunteer Action
Technology Exchange
Tools for Self Reliance
Womankind Worldwide
World Solar Programme

Renewable energy
British Association of Biofuels and Oils
British Hydropower Association
British Photovoltaic Association
British Wind Energy Association

Centre for Renewable and Sustainable Technology (CREST)
CADDETT
Croissant Neuf
Combined Heat and Power Association
Ecotricity
Energy and Environment Research Unit
Institute for Applied Ecology
Institute of Energy
Irish Energy Centre
Irish Wind Energy Association
Midlands Renewable Energy Technology Transfer
Network for Alternative Technology and Technology Assessment
New and Renewable Energy Enquiries Bureau
Renew North
Renewable Energy in the Urban Environment
Rocky Mountain Institute
SHINE 21
Solar Century
Solar Design Company
Solar Energy Centre, Southampton University
Solar Trade Association
South Midlands Renewable Energy Action Advice Centre
UK International Solar Energy Society

Energy conservation and waste minimisation

Association for the Conservation of Energy
Centre for Research Education and Training in Energy
Centre for Sustainable Energy
Community Composting Network
Community Recycling Network
Energy Systems Trade Association
Environ
Environment Technology Best Practice Programme
Environment, Energy and Waste Directorate
External Wall Insulation Association

National Energy Foundation
The Energy Savings Trust
Waste Management Information Bureau
Waste Watch

Engineering
Engineering and Marine Training Authority
Engineering Council
Institute of Chemical Engineers
Institute of Civil Engineers
Institute of Electrical Engineers
Institute of Materials
Institute of Mechanical Engineers
Institute of Incorporated Engineers

Environmental
The Environment Council
Studentforce for Sustainability
Centres for Change
Environmental Information Service
Social Venture Network Europe
Northern Ireland Environmental Link
Black Environment Network

Loans and grants
Association of British Credit Unions
Association of Community Trusts and Foundations
Association of MBAs
Aston Reinvestment Trust
Biotechnology and Biological Sciences Research Council
British Federation of Women Graduates
Career Development Loans
Department for Education and Employment
Department of Education for Northern Ireland
Ecology Building Society

Economic and Social Research Council
Educational Grant Advisory Service
Engineering and Physical Research Council
English Partnerships Community Investment
Environment Wales
Ethical Investment Research Service
ICOF Community Capital
Institution of Electrical Engineers
Local Investment Fund
Material Research Council
National Bureau for Students with Disabilities
National Union of Students
Particle Physics and Astronomy Research Council
Prospects
Shell Better Britain Campaign
Student Awards Agency for Scotland
Student Loans Company Limited
The British Academy
The Directory of Social Change
The Prince's Youth Business Trust
The Social Investment Fund
Triodos Bank
UK Social Investment Forum
Unity Trust Bank PLC
Welsh Office Education Department

Mail order book companies and publishers

Broadleys
Central Bureau for Educational Visits and Exchanges
Centre for Alternative Technology Publications
Eco-logic Books
Gaia Books
Green Books
HDRA
Hobsons

Royal Botanical Gardens Kew
Rural Agricultural and Allied Workers,
    Transport and General Workers Union
Royal Horticultural Society
Scottish Federation of Community Food Initiatives
Sunseed Tanzania Trust
Sunseed Trust
Sustain - The Alliance for Better Food and Farming
The Soil Association
The Vegan Organic Network (VOHAN)
Willing Workers on Organic Farms (WWOOF)

Places to Visit

Bath Environmental Centre
Bishops Wood Environmental Education Centre
Centre for Alternative Technology (CAT)
Earth Balance
Earth Centre
Ecological Village Project
EcoTech Centre
Energy 21 Renewable Energy Park
Henry Doubleday Research Association (HDRA)
Hockerton Housing Project
Middle Wood Trust
Natural Surroundings Centre for Wildlife Gardening
Plants for a Future
Sherwood Energy Village
Sonairte
The Eco Centre
The Eco-House
The Greenhouse Energy Centre
Woodland Fun Show

Positive economics

Co-operative Union Ltd
Action with Communities in Rural England
Asset Democracy
Association of British Credit Unions
Association of Community Trusts and Foundations
British Urban Regeneration Association
Campaign for Community Banking Services
Co-operative Union Ltd
Communes Network
Community Action Network
Community Business Scotland
Community Development Foundation
Community Enterprise Wales
Employee Ownership Scotland Ltd
Federation of Small Businesses
ICOF Community Capital
Industrial Common Ownership Finance
Industrial Common Ownership Movement (ICOM)
Irish League of Credit Unions
LETS Link Scotland
LETS Northern Ireland
Local Exchange Trading Schemes (LETS) Link
LETS Solutions
New Economics Foundation
Northern Ireland Co-operative Development
Radical Routes
Rootstock
Rural Development Commission
School for Social Entrepreneurs
Social Enterprise London
Tear Fund
The Co-operative Development Agency
The Sustainable Communities Agencies
Traidcraft Exchange

UK Co-operative Bank plc
UKSIF (Social Investment Fund)
Welsh Co-operative Development and Training Centre
Welsh Development Agency

Transport

Car Sharing
Environmental Transport Association
Sustrans
The Community Transport Association
Transport 2000

Volunteering

British Volunteer Agency Liaison Group
Central Bureau for Educational Visits and Exchanges
Community Service Volunteers
Directory of Social Change
National Association of Volunteer Bureaux
National Centre for Volunteering
National Coalition for Black Volunteering
National Council for Voluntary Organisations
Northern Ireland Volunteer Development Agency
Returned Volunteer Action
Volprof
Voluntary Service Overseas (VSO)
Volunteer Development Scotland
Wales Council for Voluntary Action/Cygnar
    Gweithnedu Gwirfeddol Cymru Llyslfor

Start your career with CAT

The Centre for Alternative Technology offers a wide range of services to help you sort out your career.

- **Visit us!** OK, mid-Wales is not the easiest of places to get to but a day's visit will set you up with ideas, inspiration and enthusiasm.

- Visit our website **www.cat.org.uk** winner of the Medianatura Best Environmental Website award it is easy to use and contains pages of valuable information.

- Check out our **mail-order** service. The books we publish and sell will help your career. They are informative and practical and will give you the in-depth information you need.

- Obtain our **resource guides**. They are comprehensive directories of companies working in the field of sustainability. The contacts you need to get on.

- Come as a **volunteer** and learn about sustainable technology first hand. Six months or one week. New Deal and NVQ potential for six month volunteers.

- Attend one of our **weekend courses**. Discounts available for students and the low waged. We host the biggest range of short courses in sustainable technologies and crafts in Britain, taught by many of Britain's leading experts.

- **Join** the Alternative Technology Association and keep up with the news.

CAT Publications:
Sustainable Environmental Solutions

Also available from CAT Publications – order form on the back page. For a full list of publications send an A5 SAE.

Architecture and building

The Whole House Book: Ecological building design and materials £29.95
Pat Borer & Cindy Harris
'*Compulsory reading for every self-builder*' Self Build and Design Magazine
'*I had a problem putting it down…a wealth of information*' British Institute of Architectural Technologists
For architects, builders and self-builders, this is the complete reference tool. Use it as a guide when choosing materials and designs, and when building. 320pp
ISBN 1 898049 79 3

Renewable energy

Windpower Workshop: Building your own wind turbine £10.00
Hugh Piggott
'Every so often books come through that are a refreshing change from the norm…Windpower Workshop is just such a book' Electronics and Beyond
'*The author is a true guru of the art*' Positive News
It's extremely satisfying to create your own power from a natural resource. This book explains very clearly the nature of wind turbines, how to make them from scrap materials, the nature of the wind resource, economic and safety issues, how to find and reuse generators and everything else you will need to construct your own. 160pp
ISBN 1 898049 20 3

Off the Grid: Managing independent renewable electricity systems £7.99
P Allen & R Todd
How to design, install and look after small-scale, renewable energy systems and live unplugged from the Grid! From system design to resource evalution for wind, hydro and solar, battery storage systems to control systems and monitoring. 60pp
ISBN 1 898049 09 2

Ecological sewage treatment and water conservation

Lifting the Lid: An ecological approach to toilet systems £10.00
Peter Harper & Louise Halestrap
'*Preconceptions about the toilet are flushed away by this book!... A fascinating read*' Positive News
Put on a pedestal for so long, the mighty WC has never been more open to challenge than it is today. This book looks at the alternatives to the flush toilet (including the compost toilet), how to manage your household's output of sewage, conserve water and turn a potential pollutant into a nutrient for use in improving the environment in a domestic or small-scale situation. 160pp
ISBN 1 898049 79 3

Sewage Solutions: Answering the call of nature £10.00
Nick Grant, Mark Moodie & Chris Weedon
Sewage can be a source of nutrients to feed soil and plants. Whether you are connected to the mains or not, this book helps you make the best choices for small-scale sewage treatment – dealing safely with the sewage of up to about 50 people. 192pp
ISBN 1 898049 16 5

Organic growing

Creative Sustainable Gardening £12.99
Diana Anthony
A book for all those gardeners wishing to improve their soil, crops and ornamental plants without harming the environment in the process. Full of practical advice and alternatives to toxic chemicals - with recipes for

soil drenches, foliar feeds and natural pesticides. Includes chapters on what it means to garden sustainably; companion planting; benign pest, disease and weed control; no-soil gardening; drought resistant gardens; low maintenance gardens and landscaping with trees. *Creative Sustainable Gardening* is a comprehensive guide to healthy gardens and a healthy future for the wider environment. Illustrated in full colour throughout. 192pp
ISBN 1 898049 23 8

CAT also publishes a range of Resource Guides to accompany the above titles, covering subjects from solar water heating, sanitation and windpower to organic growing and environmental building. There are 15 titles in all, priced between £1.00 and £3.00. Each guide contains a directory of relevant organisations, suppliers, manufacturers, books and magazines with full contact details.

For a complete publications list and an order form please contact the Mail Order Department at CAT.

CAT Mail Order Form

For ordering items listed as being available from us, ONLY! Please check to avoid disappointment.

Please cut out or photocopy and send this form (with a continuation sheet if necessary) to:

Mail Order, CAT, Machynlleth, Powys SY20 9AZ. Please write in capitals.

A complete catalogue of environmental books and products, **'Buy Green By Mail'**, is available on request for five first-class stamps.

You can phone or fax credit card orders to us on **01654 703409** (24 hours).

email. mail.order@cat.org.uk **Website.** www.cat.org.uk

CAT Publications	Quantity	Price	Total
	Total		
	Add postage and packing (see chart below)		
	Donation towards the work of CAT Charity (Thank You.) (charity number 265239)		
	Membership of the Alternative Technology Association (£14.00)		
	GRAND TOTAL		

U.K. postage and packing rates as of January 2000 until further notice	• Goods total below £10 — add £1.75 • Goods total £10.01-£20 — add £3.50 • Goods total £20.01-£40 — add £4.00 • Goods total over £40.00 — add £4.50	**Ordering overseas Postage & Packing** Europe, including Republic of Ireland - add 15% of total order for p+p. (minimum £2.00) Rest of the world - add 30% of total order for p+p. (minimum £3.00)

Title .... Initials .... Surname ....

Address ....

....

Postcode .... Tel. ....

I enclose a cheque/p.o. made out to C.A.T. ☐

Please debit my Visa/Access/Mastercard/Connect/Switch ☐

Card number .... Signature ....

Expiry date .... Issue no. .... Date ....